BACKTRACKING AROUND

FRIARY, LAIRA AND THE PLYM

then now

written & compiled by

Bernard Mills

British Library Cataloguing in Publication Data
Mills, Bernard –
Backtracking Around: Friary, Laira and the Plym
1. England - Devon - Plymouth - History
2. Railroads - England - Plymouth Region - History - 20th century ;
3. Railroads - England - Plymouth Region - History - 20th century - Pictorial works ;
Dewey: 385.0942358

I. Title
647.9'5'0942358
ISBN 978 - 0 - 9569858 - 4 - 2

Designed by Ben Robinson
Cover design by James Robinson

First published November 2013

OTHER SIMILAR TITLES FROM PEN & INK:

Plymouth Then & Now - 2004
Then & Now: The Changing Face of Plymouth - 2006
Then & Now: Plymouth - An Ever Evolving City - 2009

Published by
Pen & Ink Publishing
34 New Street
Barbican
Plymouth PL1 2NA
01752 228120

www.chrisrobinson.co.uk

Printed & bound in Great Britain by
Latimer Trend & Company Ltd
Estover Close
Plymouth PL6 7PL
Devon

Introduction

One of the last of the Laira 'Castles' 4-6-0 7022 'Hereford Castle' standing on Platform 5 awaiting departure with the 1500 to Penzance. Steam heading west from Plymouth was something that was not going to happen for much longer. The carmine and cream livery of the early 1950s carried by the leading vehicle had by this time become somewhat scarce adding to the interest. *01 June 1963*

Monday 27 July 1964 is not in any way a significant date in history, unless one is a Parliamentarian, for on this day Winston Churchill made his last appearance in the House of Commons. Far away from the Palace of Westminster, on that same day I joined the Railway as a 17-year-old young lad just out of school. I reported at 0900 to Ted Savory, the then current, and, as it transpired, the last, Station Master at Plymouth Station. His successor, Bernard Yandell, who took over on Easter Monday 1965, was appointed the first Area Manager looking after also Millbay, Friary and Tavistock Junction Marshalling Yard. One of the first of countless organisational and managerial changes I was to witness over my railway career. I retired from full time working 44 years to the day that I joined, in 2008. In that time I only ever took 12 days sick leave – and I was one of the smokers. I still do a bit of part time work for the firm, working between Totnes and Dawlish on a zero hours contract, which suits both parties and I am very happy with it.

This book does not set out to be a history of the railways of Plymouth, this is a subject that would be a veritable tome in its own right, and anyway it has all been recorded elsewhere.

Where relevant, I have quoted necessary dates in the captions to the pictures. I have set this book essentially to cover the period that I have known the system, which began with train spotting days in the 1950s, although much of the material is from the early 1960s onwards, when, at last, I could afford a decent camera. Considering that the Plymouth & Dartmoor Railway opened its line from Sutton Pool to King Tor on 26 September 1823, this represents about one quarter of the era of railways in the City of Plymouth to date.

It can be very rewarding, and indeed eye-opening, to re-visit the original locations and see how some have changed little and others almost beyond recognition. In recent outings to specifically update pictures, there are four main enemies I encountered: excessive natural growth; palisade fencing; new roads with non-stop traffic and the health and safety culture - which can be a bit over the top. But it is all good fun. I didn't meet with a single refusal for access to property to update the images. I did however get a few strange looks, for example, when I was standing in the middle of Plymstock roundabout, and a look of total disbelief when standing on the Barbican Approach outside the Thistle Brewhouse, in the middle of the road, explaining I was trying to update a picture I once took from a train here.

The bulk of the illustrations are my own work. I have been very fortunate to have use of the colour pictures taken by my great friend and early mentor Ivor Hocking, made possible by the digital restoration of the original slides - ten years in a garden shed did not do them much good! I have also been able to use a few taken by another great friend, the late Keith Holt through the good offices of his son Alistair. The rest are made up from my own collection where I hold the copyright. Where pictures used are not from my own resources, these are individually acknowledged in the caption.

So come with me on an imaginary journey east from Plymouth Station out around the Lipson Curve and on to Sutton Harbour. Then enjoy exploring Friary, its shed and the complex lines that radiated from there. Back then to examine Laira Shed, the Causeway and on out to Plympton.

Although the Tavistock Branch is really beyond the scope of this book, and will hopefully have its own volume in due course, I have stretched a point and included that part of it which lay in Plymouth, and has become the 'jewel in the crown' of the system due to its restoration from nothing by the Plym Valley Railway. Their achievements cannot be overstated enough.

My thanks to the many who have helped me in many ways in preparation of this book, I must mention especially Mike Hunt, David Mitchell, Mike Woodhouse, Arthur Westington, John Netherton, Tony Kingdom, Steve and Ron Andrews, and Roger Geach who have responded to all my requests for information, and trying to refresh the memory. I am grateful to Stuart Hammond for touching up some of the photos, and my drinking partner Jeremy Clark for putting me right on the vagrancies of using Microsoft Word. Finally to series editor Chris Robinson and his team for producing this book, my thanks for their encouragement and faith in me to get it off the ground.

Should you wish to purchase any of the photographs contained in this book and many, many more from my collection as a digital download to enjoy on your own computer or obtain a quality print, go to:
http://.classictractionimages.weebly.com

The Plymouth Railway Circle is mentioned widely in this book, this vibrant Society is still going strong and meetings are held on alternate Mondays - September to May - at St. Edward's Church Hall, Home Park Avenue, Peverell, Plymouth, commencing at 1930, and there are still outings in the Summer, often with a special train. For more information go to:
http://plymouthrailwaycircle.weebly.com

For those wishing to gain practical railway experience, to get involved with stock and other restoration work or just be a part of the team preserving the steam and golden age of railways in the City, look no further than the Plym Valley Railway at Marsh Mills, call in any Sunday to see them, or go to:
http://www.plymrail.co.uk

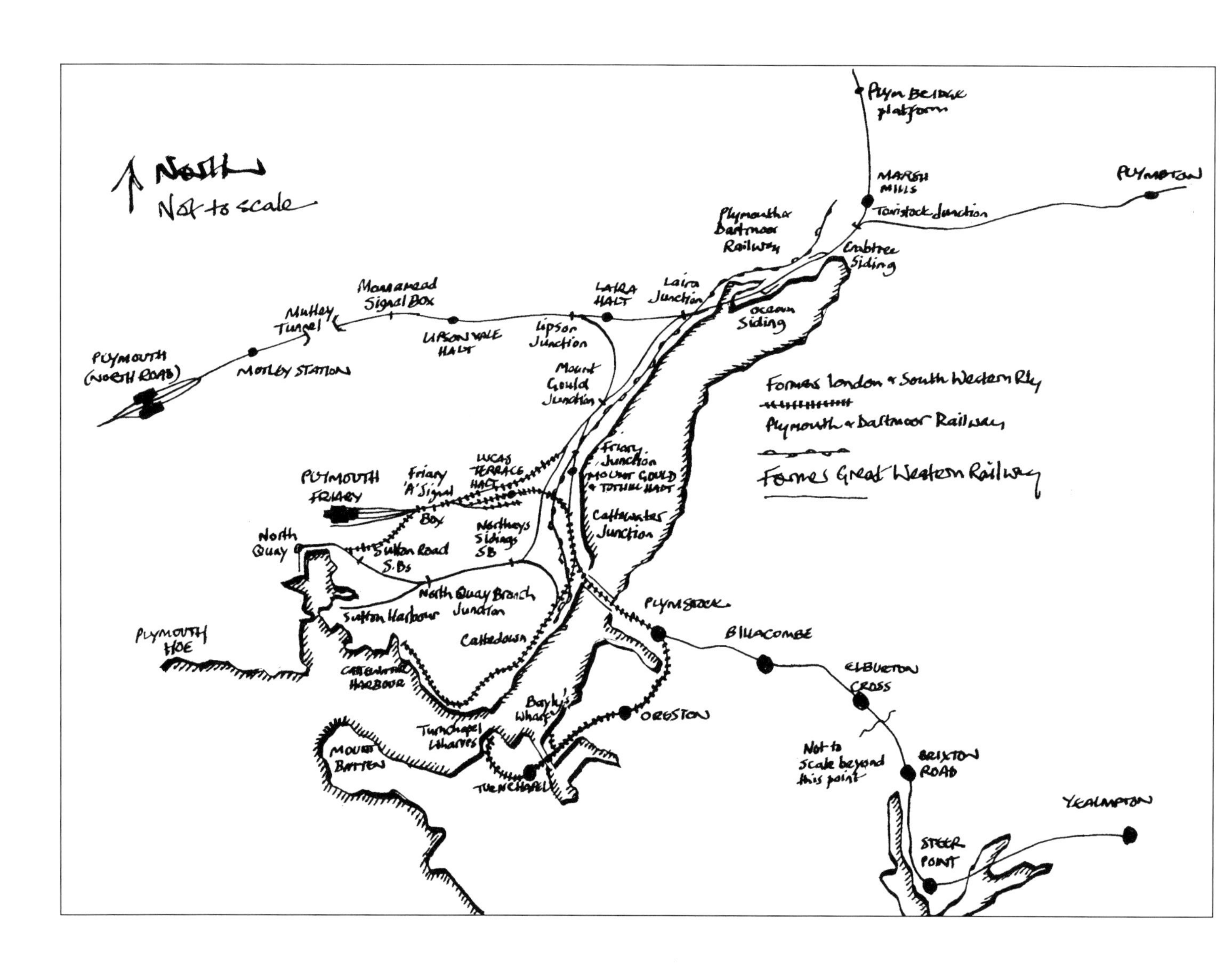

BACKTRACKING AROUND
FRIARY, LAIRA AND THE PLYM

The dawn of the diesels when all that really changed was the engine on the front of the train and everything else carried on as before, the fireman who was now becoming known as the second man is attaching the 'Cornish Riviera Express' headboard to the front of 'Warship' D811 'Daring'. *August 1962*

Contents

PLYMOUTH STATION – PLATFORMS 2 AND 3

We commence our look at the railways of Plymouth at the former Plymouth North Road station. The North Road suffix was dropped on the closure to Friary to passengers on 15 September 1958.

ABOVE: The 1962 station has altered little over the years, although Platforms 2 and 3 have. They are seen here looking east towards Mutley with both Southern and Great Western motive power on show reflecting the former joint use of the station. The photographer, my great friend the late Keith Holt, is standing on Platform 2 and in platform 3, 'N' class 2-6-0 31874 awaits departure with the 1918 To Exeter Central via Okehampton, the train known as 'The Mail'. Behind on Platform 4 GWR 'Prairie' 4555 is engaged on station pilot duties. Remarkably, both engines are still with us. 31874 is currently on the Mid Hants Railway awaiting overhaul, and 4555 can be found at the not too far away Dartmouth Steam Railway. *30 April 1963*

BELOW: In the 1974 track alteration scheme, platforms 2 and 3 were abolished as through lines, a covered walkway being constructed more or less at their mid point to create four bay platforms. The two at the eastern end were given over to parcels and mail train use and see little activity at the present time. At the west end, the former Platform 2 became known as 'Dock 4' and has generally been used for stabling purposes. Platform 3 became a bay platform mainly for use by the Gunnislake branch services and was the only one of the four bays adapted and signalled for passenger train use. 'Sprinter' 150 120 has just arrived with the 1345 from Gunnislake. *21 August 2013*

PLYMOUTH STATION EAST END, THE TRANSITION YEARS

Without doubt one of the greatest upheavals on the railway in the era I have known was the transition from steam to diesel. The first diesel shunter arrived at Friary Shed in March 1957. Just about a year later the first main line diesel arrived at Laira and the first diesel multiple unit was seen later that year. Steam had all but disappeared from the former Western Region lines by the close of 1963 and finished on the former Southern lines in September 1964. The last operational steam engine was seen in April 1965.

TOP: Steam and diesel combinations over the South Devon Banks were a common sight, in those few years the two forms of power existed side by side in the area. As far as I know, this is the last occasion a 'King' Class 4-6-0 worked a timetabled train from Paddington, although there was a later last fling when they were involved with football specials bringing Tottenham Hotspur supporters down for a Third Round FA Cup Tie. 6021 'King Richard II' and D6323 make their way out to Laira Shed after working a train from London, the diesel had been attached at Newton Abbot. *September 1961*

MIDDLE: A similar combination when steam was getting a little thin on the ground, D6327 pilots 'Castle' 4-6-0 5057 'Earl Waldegrave' into Platform 2 with a Paddington to Penzance train, the diesel having been attached at Newton Abbot. *1 June 1963*

BOTTOM: Since the track alterations of 1974, 'down' passenger trains can no longer use Platform 2. Representing the final transition from locomotive-hauled trains to full operation by fixed-formation units, the uniquely liveried 57 601 - then on hire to First Great Western - arrives at platform 4 with 5C50 1923 Exeter St Davids - Plymouth empty stock. Other than the disappearance of the red stock used for the mail trains, until the contract was lost to rail in January 2004, the scene has changed little with the houses in Glen Park Road being the common link between the pictures. *22 June 2001*

THE THROUGH ROAD WITH STEAM AND DIESEL

The 'through' road between Platforms 4 and 5 at Plymouth Station has always been of advantage for operational reasons. In the days of locomotive-hauled trains, it was particularly useful for either the incoming or outgoing locomotive to use without blocking up a platform. Today the odd HST Power Car may do the same if an en route change is required. Trains such as freight or ballast/engineering trains requiring to be passed by passenger trains still occasionally use the facility.

ABOVE: Having been detached from its train from London, 'Castle' Class 4-6-0 5057 'Earl Waldegrave' runs tender first along the 'Through' Road to await the signal to proceed to Laira Depot. Its lengthy train is still at Platform 2 where a diesel has taken over for the onward run to Penzance, the engine seeming to attract much interest from the passengers if the number of heads out of the window is anything to go by! *1 June 1963*

BELOW: One train which was booked to terminate in the 'Through' road was 1215 Bristol Temple Meads-Plymouth empty vans. With the more modern station names board in place, 'Class 47' diesels 47 733 and 47 741 make an impressive sight as they arrive with this working, the train at this time booked for two locomotives for balancing purposes. These workings finished in January 2004 and like 5057 going to Laira, they too are a memory and a reminder of the varied trains once seen in the City. A much higher elevation of this location follows on the next page. *1 September 1997*

PLYMOUTH STATION FROM TOWER BLOCK FOURTH FLOOR LOOKING EAST

A slightly higher elevation looking down on the east end of the station from the fourth floor of the Tower Block, in camera terms we have 'zoomed out' from the pictures on the previous page of 5057 and the double-headed Class 47 van trains which were taken on the east end of Platform 4, the nearest through platform to the right of the scene. The Tower Block was opened by Dr Beeching in March 1962. This effectively marked the completion of the rebuilding of the Station which had actually commenced way back in 1939, the work being interrupted by the Second World War. The scheme was revived in 1956, under the British Railways Modernisation Plan (of 1955), giving us the station we are so familiar with today some 50 years or so on. One major change in the intervening years has been the track rationalisation scheme of the Spring-early Summer 1974, and this is clearly reflected in the two images.

ABOVE: An unidentified 'Peak' waits to depart with a north-bound cross-country train. Notice the Civil Engineer's Inspection Saloon parked in the 'down' sidings on the right, the considerable amount of activity with the former 'National Carriers' trailers in the Parcels Yard and the motorail van with its doors open awaiting its next customer. *April 1970*

RIGHT: 43041 and 43129 are seen leaving the station with 1A83 1000 Penzance - Paddington and a few things have changed over the years. Much of the former 'down' sidings and the Parcels Yard have become the staff car park and the canopy over the former Platform 2 and the Parcels Bay was removed between May and August 2012. This has, in part, been replaced by a rather more flimsy looking structure as part of the accommodation block for the Station Offices. Off the rails, the view of the surrounding area looks very similar with one notable exception. On the right-hand skyline, the spire of Mutley Methodist Church, demolished in 1977, has vanished. *21 August 2013*

PLYMOUTH NORTH ROAD STATION EAST

The two pictures are broadly similar with the common link being the houses of Glen Park Road and the back lane to the left, the latter a place where numerous train spotters have spent many happy hours over the years.

ABOVE: 'M7' 30036 is seen departing for Laira Carriage Sidings with the empty stock off the 1730 Brentor to Plymouth. The view is from the steps of the former North Road East Signal Box, the background dominated by the Station Tower Block under construction. *September 1961*

BELOW: A slightly different elevation for a more recent view, the site of the former North Road East Signal Box demolished in March 2003 is in the foreground, the fence and the relay room preclude a precise update from the same angle. 'Adelante' Units 180 110 leading and 180 104 on the rear are seen arriving with 1C89 1435 Paddington - Plymouth on 2 August 2004, the first appearance of the class in the City. The view has altered little in the last decade. *2 August 2004*

SUTHERLAND ROAD BRIDGE LOOKING WEST

A quick glance at the three pictures reveals the view is pretty much the same, with the Station Buildings, the Tower Block and the spires of the Roman Catholic Cathedral and St Peter's Church in Wydham Square being the obvious reference points. In the 43-year time-span covering the scene, there have been some subtle changes. The one which stands out of course is the track work, simplified in the alteration scheme of the summer of 1974. Another change to the railway scene is the rather sad, empty, modern-day look at the station, due to loss of traffic, like the milk trains that finished in August 1979, and the GPO Mail, in January 2004. No need for these vehicles to be berthed in the sidings. The lighting pylons in the Park Sidings have been modernised, and the other major change is the former GPO Sorting Office in Pennycomequick in the far right back ground, which nowadays has become the site for yet another student accommodation block.

RIGHT: Class 47 D1584 pulls away with the 1120 Plymouth - Manchester. *18 May 1970*

RIGHT: 'Voyager' 221 130 is seen with the 0825 Penzance-Dundee. Even this is now history as Virgin Trains, rather surprisingly, lost the Cross Country franchise in November 2007. *27 March 2007*

RIGHT: 'Voyager' 220 027 arriving with 1V46 0632 from York. As well as the livery change for the train, there are a few minor changes since 2007, the most notable being growth on the bank to the left, another pylon light has sprung up rather spoiling the outline of the Tower Block and the recent changes to the canopy on what was once Platform 2. *21 August 2013*

STEAM AT SUTHERLAND ROAD BRIDGE

BELOW: Apsley Road was a favourite place for the local railway enthusiasts to gather on a summer's evening as there would always be plenty to see, usually with something of interest. The entrance to the former North Road East Signal Box had a convenient gap in the line side fence, and the authorities were quite happy to turn a blind eye as long as people were sensible and no one went on to the track. A smart-looking 'Modified Hall' 4-6-0, No 7909 'Heveningham Hall' heads under the bridge light engine for Laira Shed after working an 'Up' service from Penzance. *September 1961*

BELOW: Nowadays few people gather here on a summer's, or indeed any other, evening due to the high palisade fencing spoiling the view, and with just the daily diet of High Speed Trains, Cross Country Voyagers and Sprinters, there is precious little of interest to see anyway. A few may gather here to watch the odd steam-hauled rail tour. Of course access through the fence to obtain a line side shot in the same position now would almost require an Act of Parliament, so for a more recent view of a steam engine in the same place, we move on to Sutherland Road Bridge for a very rare morning departure east out of Plymouth Station with 'Black 5' 4-6-0 no 45407 with 5Z23 1040 Empty Coaching Stock to Tavistock Junction. Look behind the tender and one can see what I mean about the fencing now blocking the view. Both engines are in the same place, it is just a different view point for the images taken, believe it or not, some 46 years apart. *27 March 2007*

SUTHERLAND ROAD BRIDGE LOOKING EAST

Looking east from Sutherland Road Bridge on the south side, the view has hardly altered over the years: the dominant feature being the Royal Eye Infirmary which closed in January 2013. The main changes occur in the period between the top two pictures. The spire of the former Mutley Methodist Church demolished in 1977 no longer rises above the houses, and on the railway the track and point layout was altered in the 1974 scheme. Something that does change in all four pictures is the traffic parked in Apsley Road, still bi-directional in 1984, a chance to study the road vehicles over four decades or so.

TOP: 'Peak' D89 brings in the Plymouth attachment consisting of a splendid former Southern Region PMV – Parcels Miscellaneous Van, the buffet car and additional coaches, from Laira for the 'Up' 'Cornishman' from Penzance to Bradford. Interesting to note the changes in the passenger train service. Back in 1970 one could count on the fingers of one hand the number of through trains to the North East. Today under the Cross Country Franchise an hourly service runs that way from 0523 to 1725. *18 May 1970*

BENEATH: The trees to the right of the Eye Infirmary appear to have been pollarded at the time. On the rails, Plymouth has, since 1979, entered the High Speed Train era. This is not Inter City 725, forget the passengers and run a lightweight train. Now and then Power Cars have occasionally to be changed in the Station. Here a pair return to Laira Depot after such a move. Another memory of course is the attractive British Rail livery they first carried. *February 1984*

RIGHT: Seventeen years on from the 1984 view and little has changed, except for the traffic parked up in Apsley Road, which is now one way. The Eye Infirmary has gained a few more modern NHS signs, and the trees have grown. 'Standard 4' 76079 is captured running out to Laira to turn on the triangle having worked a 'South Devon Coastal' special from Exeter. *5 August 2001*

BOTTOM: Bringing the story right up to date, 220 015 passes by with 1V48 0645 Newcastle-Plymouth bang on time at 1341 on 21 August 2013. Since the closure of the Eye Infirmary on 23 January 2013, parking is now not a problem in Apsley Road, but there is still a good supply of modern vehicles on display. The other change of note is the railings by the railway, a popular place with many to stand and view, in particular, the steam specials departing on their journey east. In the first week of May 2013 the old worn-out set were replaced by a set of surprisingly 'user friendly' modern black railings, which have, if anything, made life a little more comfortable for the photographers. *21 August 2013*

APSLEY ROAD LOOKING WEST

A view familiar to many over the years where the trains pull away from Plymouth Station on a rising gradient passing under Sutherland Road Bridge, dominated by the Station Tower Block in the distance. Above D1021 'Western Cavalier' is more than likely making a superb noise as she gets to grips with the 16 bogie 1M01 1600 St Austell to Kensington Olympia Motorail on 3 June 1974, Plymouth depart time 1700. This service finished at the close of the 1981 season, being replaced for three years by a separate train for the cars only from Paddington. The driver and passengers travelled on a normal service train, with the inevitable delays between the arrival of the car and the people, or vice versa, at their destination hastening the decline of the service. First Great Western revived a limited service between Paddington and Penzance from 1998 to 2005 utilising a couple of special covered vans attached to the overnight 'Night Riviera' service. Motorail is another of those trains that used to run and were once a familiar sight passing through the City.

Other than the track layout, altered during the 1974 re-signalling scheme, and some foliage on the left, the view is almost identical as 'Sprinter' 150 263 is seen heading away from Plymouth with 2M88 1644 Penzance-Taunton on *17 May 2013*

APSLEY ROAD LOOKING EAST

Countless numbers of people have stood by the railings outside the Royal Eye Infirmary to watch the trains go by, and still do when the occasional steam or other interesting rail tour passes. Another description of the view would of course be looking toward the site of the former Mutley Station. It opened 1 August 1871 when the area was still very rural, and closed 2 March 1939.

ABOVE: We go back to the early summer of 1969 for the 'then' picture which will come as a sheer delight to those who revere the rather short-lived 'Hydraulic' era as 'Western' class D1068 'Western Reliance,' in maroon livery, heads east on an early evening 'Up' train, passing 'Warship' D832 'Onslaught', which had been a recent recipient of a full yellow end, parked in the locomotive sidings. I do recall there was a notice to engine men here to keep their charges silent so as not to cause noise and disturbance to patients in the Eye Infirmary. There is a clear view of Mutley Tunnel, Ermington Terrace to the left and Gordon and Napier Terraces to the right. Mutley Baptist Church is the prominent feature of the right-hand background. *May 1969*

BELOW: The present-day picture, taken as 'Sprinter' 150 263 heads away with 2M88 1644 Penzance to Taunton, looks very familiar although there are a couple of changes of note, the main one being the concrete Mutley Car Park, built by the City Council in 1973-74 over the railway tracks. Surprisingly one of the former locomotive sidings remains in place, although it has to be said this sees little use these days. Another noticeable feature is the growth of vegetation to the right, not yet quite high enough to obscure the view of Mutley Baptist Church. *17 May 2013*

GORDON TERRACE

This was another popular place to watch the trains go by, and strolling along here you would usually see something to see on the rails These days there can be gaps of up to 15 minutes or more between moves, mostly accounted for by there being no need for the once never-ending procession of light engines to and from Laira Depot, and fewer empty stock moves, combined with the decline in freight traffic.

ABOVE: A smart-looking D1056 'Western Sultan' is heading out to Laira Depot after bringing up the 1245 Penzance-Crewe Perishables as far as Plymouth, passing the three-aspect colour-light signal 'P18' which is just about on what would have been the end of the 'down' platform of the former Mutley Station. This signal controlled the entrance to Plymouth Station for trains from the east. The square box at the top is an indicator which informed the driver which platform number (or the 'through line') for which the route is set. This signal was re-positioned in the 1974 track alteration scheme and is now situated in a very short gap immediately at the west end of Mutley Tunnel and the concrete car park of the early 1970s. *August 1968*

ABOVE: Otherwise, except for the rather excessive growth of vegetation on the railway bank, the view is much the same as seen in the right hand picture. The much loved Royal Eye Infirmary which closed in January 2013 looks just the same. One can only hope its appearance will not be altered in the changes and developments that will now surely follow. *21 August 2013*

GORDON TERRACE/NAPIER TERRACE

A little sequential train planning for the railway enthusiasts, as it is not often that consecutively numbered locomotives followed each other on successive trains.

RIGHT: For the top two pictures we go back to 14 October 1969 looking along Gordon Terrace where it runs in to Napier Terrace. In the foreground the slope which was the entrance to the 'down' platform of the former Mutley Station. To the left a few old cars can be seen in Ermington Terrace, plenty of room to park there back then, and the trains are emerging from Mutley Tunnel. Local historian Chris Robinson recalled that this is where he and his youth club chums used to watch the trains go by, another once favourite location for train spotting.

In the top picture, a rather scruffy looking D1009 'Western Invader,' still in its original maroon livery, passes by with 'The Cornishman' 1V70 0706 Bradford Exchange to Penzance, arriving in Plymouth 1455 and departing at 1508. This was followed by the now preserved (on the West Somerset Railway) D1010 'Western Campaigner', which had by then been repainted in the British Rail corporate blue livery, on an empty stock move from Laira Carriage Sidings to Plymouth Station. This is misleading since the driver had not altered the head code and it is obviously not an express heading for London! *14 October 1969*

LEFT: The third picture in this sequence is almost depressing. There is little chance that small boys, or anyone else, will gather here to watch the trains go by, such is the growth of vegetation. One can hardly see the railway and even the concrete car park over the railway, constructed in early 1970s, has been completely obscured. *21 August 2013*

IVYDALE ROAD LOOKING WEST

The section of the main line between the east end of Plymouth (North Road until 1958) Station and Lipson Junction was for many years a bottleneck. Bear in mind not only did the Great Western passenger, freight and transfer workings pass along here, all the Southern trains to and from Friary did as well, and there were of course the countless light-engine movements between Laira Shed and North Road/Millbay. Ideally the Great Western would have wished to quadruple or at least lay in a third line to give more operating flexibility, but were constrained by the 183-yard Mutley Tunnel and the topography of the area. To relieve the operating pressure, Mannamead Signal Box was opened here in 1905. This, in railway terms, is what we call a 'Block Post', the signal box did not control any points. It broke the section between North Road East and Lipson Junction Signal Boxes enabling the line capacity to be increased. Former Signalmen employed here have told me that although it was only a six lever frame, it was very rare to see all six in the normal position. In simple terms that means there was always one of the signals pulled off. The great boast, apparently, was to get the 'Down distant' in the 'off' position, usually only accomplished on a Peak Summer Saturday for the first part of the 'Cornish Riviera' from Paddington to St Ives. This busy little signal box was closed 25 March 1956 and replaced by Intermediate Block Signals, these lasting until the Plymouth Panel Box took over the area on 26 November 1960.

TOP: In the evening sunshine of 17 May 1977, the empty stock of a short-formed Royal Train is seen passing the site of the former Mannamead Signal Box, on the right. Mutley Plain is clearly visible above the tunnel, and note the 'Bowyers' vans parked up. *17 May 1979*

MIDDLE: Recalling the days of the endless procession of light locomotives to and from Laira Shed, 'Hall' 4930 'Hagley Hall' leads 'Castle' 5051 'Earl Bathurst' tender-first from Laira to Plymouth Station, where they picked up a support coach before working their way to Newton Abbot where they took over a special rail tour as part of the GWR 150th Celebrations. In the meantime, a car park has appeared on the left. *14 July 1985*

BOTTOM: The double-track railway line is still there, the buildings on Mutley Plain can just be picked out above the now obscured tunnel and the rear of the houses in Alexandra Road on the left look much the same, otherwise vegetation has taken over much of the view. 43303 brings up the rear of the Sunday 1V50 0900 Leeds-Plymouth. *28 July 2013*

IVYDALE ROAD LOOKING EAST

Three views looking east at Ivydale Road, where the background hills and the curve of the line are the most notable link. Where the line is straight, this was the site of the former Lipson Vale Halt, opened in the boom years of the suburban traffic on 1 June 1904, closed 4 May 1942 and dismantled more or less immediately due to fire risk, as the platforms were of wooden construction. It had only been used by the Southern trains since 7 July 1930 after withdrawal of the Plympton rail motors and the first Yealmpton branch passenger closure. *7 July 1930.*

TOP: 'Class 31s' 31 414 and 31 416 provide somewhat unusual motive power for the short Royal train seen going away into Mutley Tunnel on the previous page. The most notable feature to the right is the fondly remembered Bowyers factory in Alexandra Road, which closed in 1979. Its delivery vans – and the delicious produce they carried – are remembered by many. *17 May 1977*

MIDDLE: We move in to the new century, just, for a view of a rare visitor to Plymouth, the famous former London and North Eastern Railway 'A3' Class Pacific 4472 'Flying Scotsman', in its original livery but carrying a couple of modifications from its British Railways era, notably the double chimney and the German-type smoke deflectors. As far as I know, this was the first time the engine had visited the City hauling a passenger train, but, as we shall see when discussing Mount Gould Junction, not the first time the engine had reached Plymouth. 4472 on the last lap of 'The West Country Scotsman' Rail Tour promoted by St Albans Travel Service, who traded as 'Flying Scotsman Railways Limited, passing Ivydale Road with 1Z91 0717 Paddington-Plymouth ten minutes late at 1455. Note how the vegetation had grown in the intervening years, otherwise still a very recognisable scene. A minor change bottom left; the bath tubs have been removed and there is now a more substantial line side fence. *30 June 2001*

BOTTOM: Bringing the scene right up to date as 43022 and 43129 pass by with 5A29 1528 Empty Stock Laira to Plymouth Station to form the Sunday 1A29 1610 Plymouth - Paddington. The most notable changes are the vegetation especially to the left, and to the right the new 'Alexandra Works' student accommodation block, built on the site of the former Bowyers Factory, dominates the scene. Directly opposite this there is a common feature in the same place in all three pictures, namely the colour-light signal on the 'Up' line: the ghost of Mannamead Signal Box! *28 July 2013*

LIPSON NUMBER ONE CURVE

The Lipson Number One Curve from Lipson Junction on the main line to Mount Gould Junction on the then Sutton Harbour Branch was opened by the GWR on 1 April 1891. This was to allow direct access for London & South Western trains to reach Friary without a reversal at Laira Junction. The line remains in use today as part of the Laira Triangle.

ABOVE: A poignant moment as the last 'Castle' Class 4-6-0 7029 'Clun Castle' to work an express on the former GWR route out of Plymouth heads towards Lipson Junction and into the Station to pick up its train, the legendary 1Z48 1620 Plymouth--Paddington on 9 May 1964. This was indeed the swan song of steam but that is another story.

Behind the gleaming locomotive is a part of Laira Depot, the Long Shed of 1931, and, to the right, the oil tanks installed after the Second War. The houses in Efford dominate the skyline.

Overleaf:
TOP: A higher elevation on 23 September 1972 for a Plymouth Station to Laira Shed Shuttle for the Depot Open Day. The Steam Shed was closed in October 1964 and demolished two years later, the site being used for additional stock storage, also as a Civil Engineer's Depot since their relocation from Doublebois.

MIDDLE: 7029 'Clun Castle' made a welcome return on 6 September 1985 as part of the GWR 150 Celebrations, working the empty stock off 1Z47 1510 Truro - Plymouth Rail Tour out to Friary, the engine captured almost to the inch as in the May 1964 photograph. There are a few changes in the background; a few more houses have appeared on the hill behind, and the Civil Engineers no longer use the former steam shed. Notable in the stock stored is the prototype 140 'Pacer' unit partly hidden by the steam from 7029.

BOTTOM: Laira Estate looks much the same with the land marks of the School top left and St Mary The Virgin Church on the right. The Railway is still there but surrounded by high-security fencing. The former steam shed is still in use for stock storage, although there is not so much stock to store these days. Otherwise the view from the park has become a familiar story, the uncontrolled growth of vegetation has really taken over and obscured the view. *3 August 2013*

THE SPEEDWAY

To enable easier access to and from Laira Shed and to relieve the pressure on Laira Junction, a new link line from just to the south of the Coaling Stage to the Lipson Number One Curve was opened on 18 September 1931. Since this speeded up the despatch of locomotives into Plymouth Station, especially those chimney facing Paddington, the nickname 'Speedway' was bestowed, and remains in use to the present day. Railway History is rarely simple, and in respect of the Laira Triangle, and as we shall shortly see the Friary and associated areas, it is complicated and very difficult to explain simply, but bear with me and I will do my best. We have yet to explore the Sutton Harbour Branch which ran from Laira Junction alongside Embankment Road, and in railway terms by the former Laira Goods Yard (closed in 1958 to enable construction of the Diesel Depot), and through the carriage sidings. This line was closed between Laira and Mount Gould Junctions as from 02/04 June 1979, being diverted over the 'Speedway' which at the Laira Junction end was altered from being a depot siding to join the former Sutton Harbour Line for a few yards for the connection to the main line. This is thus the present day formation of the Laira Triangle for operational purposes, and is now the direct route from Laira Junction in to Friary.

Plenty to study in the top picture as a Plymouth Station to Laira Depot DMU Shuttle for the 07 September 1985 Open Day is seen on the former 'Speedway' now the Laira Junction-Mount Gould Junction route. A temporary wooden station constructed just beyond the level crossing can be seen, and this is within yards of the temporary Laira Green Terminus of 1848-49. Shades of the suburban era were recalled here this day as well, as some Laira residents actually used the temporary depot halt for going in to Plymouth to do the shopping, a rare chance indeed for local use of the railway. Of particular note the replica Broad Gauge 'Iron Duke' built especially for the 1985 celebrations can be spotted more or less where the steam shed coaling stage once stood. Note also the clear view of the Diesel Depot brought in to use 13 March 1962 and the Mullet Pond, now a nature reserve.

All the hustle and bustle has gone by the time of the middle view taken 05 April 1997 when 'King' 6024 'King Edward 1' used the triangle to turn after working a special that had originated at Birmingham International from Taunton. The former 'Speedway' does not look quite so neat and tidy, and a few more buildings have appeared in the Depot Car Park.

The third view taken 03 August 2013 really needs little comment. The growth has won the battle.

Inside Laira Depot, the former 'Speedway' commenced just to the south of the coaling stage, seen here behind 7029 'Clun Castle', coming off shed ready to work the Ian Allan 1Z48 1620 Plymouth--Paddington 9 May 1964. As already seen, on reaching the Lipson Number One Curve, the engine would simply reverse for the run in to the Station. This is an historic picture for, as far as I know, as this was the last 'Castle' off Laira, and the shed would close to steam just five months later. I remember standing there as a young 17-year-old lad trying to take it all in, a wonderful occasion to witness.

ABOVE: The angle is different, but the engines are in exactly the same place. Taken from the public footpath that runs from Mount Gould Park to Laira, the Lipson Number One Curve is in the foreground, and the diversion and extension of the 'Speedway' towards Laira Junction can be clearly identified. Taken on 12 October 2002, the growth is taking over but the Diesel Depot of March 1962 is still visible as another distinguished visitor ex London Midland and Scottish Railway 4-6-2 'Coronation' Class Pacific 6233 'Duchess of Sutherland' turns on the Laira Triangle.

ABOVE: A third variation of a train in more or less the same place on the 'Speedway' taken from a different angle. A shuttle from Plymouth Station formed with the unique Class 116 DMU painted in 'British Telecom' advertising livery approaches the temporary platform for the Open Day at Laira Depot on 7 September 1985. The picture above of 6233 here was taken from the Park seen in the background.

ABOVE: Same spot, but a fourth variation of the angle as seen on 26 October 2012. Due to the excessive growth, I elected to stand on the opposite side of the track to where the Telecom Unit was pictured in 1985.

MOUNT GOULD JUNCTION

This is where the Lipson Number One Curve of April 1891 met the Sutton Harbour Branch from Laira Junction which had opened in 1853.

TOP: The 'Flying Scotsman,' on its brief first visit to the City on 21 September 1973, is indeed a rare and distinguished visitor to what was the Sutton Harbour Branch. After a season working on the Torbay and Dartmouth Railway, the engine came down on its own just to turn on the Laira triangle. The view is from the park at Mount Gould, overlooking the Junction as 4472 heads towards Laira Junction, the former footbridge which gave pedestrian access to the Diesel Depot can just be spotted on the right with the signals that were once worked from Mount Gould Junction Signal Box. A notable feature of the picture is the amount of traffic on the Embankment on a Friday afternoon!

MIDDLE: A slightly different viewpoint from Mount Gould Park as a fairly new High Speed Train built for the Cross County Service (only one first-class vehicle) with Power Cars 43172 and 43171 approach Mount Gould Junction from Lipson Junction with a shuttle for the Laira Depot Open Day on 25 April 1982. There have been a few changes in the intervening years; the area was taken over by the Plymouth Panel Signal Box on 10 November 1973, and the layout into the Depot was altered when the 'Speedway' was adapted as the normal route for through trains from the east towards Friary. The footbridge was removed as part of this scheme. The normal route today for the High Speed Trains to and from Laira Depot and Plymouth Station involves a reversal at Mount Gould Junction.

BOTTOM: A combination of high fencing in Mount Gould Park and excessive growth make a modern-day comparison almost impossible. This was only achieved on 3 August 2013 by returning for a second time to update the pictures by bringing along a little set of portable steps. Yes, the railway is still down in the cutting, but one would never know it today. It is the River Plym in the background which really links all three pictures.

MOUNT GOULD JUNCTION

ABOVE: A meeting at Mount Gould! A probably rare and interesting combination as 4472 'Flying Scotsman' heads away from Mount Gould Junction towards Laira Junction and passes Class 25 D7575 (later 25 225) heading for Friary with the afternoon goods. The Class 25 Diesels had a fairly short life in the Plymouth area, D7573, D7575 and D7577 were transferred to Laira Depot from the London Midland Region in October 1971, this being part of a large British Rail fleet re-organisation as the Diesel Hydraulic fleet was being decimated. The 25s were not popular in the West Country, their mechanical condition left a lot to be desired, but as things improved they became good workhorses over the local system. Re-numbered as 25 225 in 1974, the engine was withdrawn in October 1980, bringing an end to Class 25 activity in the area, and was cut up at Swindon Works the following month. 4472 has fortunately fared much better, and despite many problems is still with us now as part of the National Collection. *21 September 1973*

ABOVE: It was only by walking along the fence in Mount Gould Park and every few yards standing on my little portable steps and peering over the growth that I found the landmark to link the two pictures, the Plymouth Amateur Rowing Club building. The railway and the never-ending stream of traffic along Embankment Road are still there as well, it is just that it is all hidden by the excessive vegetation. *3 August 2013*

MOUNT GOULD JUNCTION

Three views of Mount Gould junction where the main link is the background of the Laira Bridge and the hills beyond. This is where the Lipson Number One Curve met the Sutton Harbour Branch.

TOP: A DMU waits at Mount Gould Junction on the Lipson Number One Curve awaiting permission to proceed. A panorama showing the houses and the Signal Box, a relatively traffic-free Embankment Road and, in the distance, Plymstock Cement Works shows up well on the left, Laira Bridge in the middle and the former Power Station to the right. The DMU will reverse here to gain access to Laira Shed, a move still performed daily by trains to and from the Depot. *23 September 1972*

MIDDLE: although only taken a year later, there has been one small change and that is the track work where the line leading from the Lipson Number One Curve was singled on 3 June 1973. The signal at which the DMU was standing in the top picture lays forlorn on the ground in the 'V' of the two lines. 4472 'Flying Scotsman' having rounded the Lipson Number One Curve has reversed and is setting off for Laira Junction and points east. *1 September 1973*

BOTTOM: A precise updated view is not possible, so I have had to stand on the Park side of the fence, yet again vegetation has made a great impact on the scene obliterating the view of the railway and the now much busier Embankment Road. Laira Bridge provides the main link in a much changed background. *3 August 2013*

LANHYDROCK ROAD BRIDGE LOOKING EAST

ABOVE: Plenty of activity at Mount Gould Junction as 'Peak' D127 pauses on 10 June 1973 with 8Z91 Laira to Friary engineering train. Mount Gould Signal Box can be spotted in the background where the steam crane seems to be employed on track renewal, the park used for the photographs on the previous page is in the middle distance on the left. To the right was the line of the Plymouth & Dartmoor Tramway of 1823, this was later absorbed by the Lee Moor Tramway and closed finally in 1961. The allotments form a nice open space leading to the view of Embankment Road.

BELOW: Much has changed in the intervening years; the line on which D127 is standing originally, the 'Down' Main to nearby Friary Junction, has since become the carriage-washing plant for Laira Depot installed in 1981, trains for Friary use the left-hand line. Mount Gould Junction Signal Box was closed on 10 November 1973 when the Plymouth Panel Signal Box took over the area, the park top left as we have already discovered is obscured by foliage but in contrast, an amazing array of little sheds and buildings have appeared in the ever-popular allotments. Trees hide the busy Embankment Road. *24 June 2012*

LANHYDROCK ROAD LOOKING WEST, FRIARY JUNCTION

A picture supplied by Ron Andrews through Classic Traction taken track side and one full of interest. This is Friary Junction where the London and South Western Railway (later the Southern Railway) regained its own metals with the double-track line to the right curving away to the terminus at Friary. The signal box here closed on 29 September 1959. The line going straight on is the one we are going to follow, the Great Western Branch to Sutton Harbour which was closed beyond this point 03 December 1973 and demolished the following September. To the left the Plymouth & Dartmoor, later the Lee Moor, Tramway ran parallel. The black bridge over the Sutton Harbour Branch is the Southern Branch from Friary to Cattewater and Plymstock and the next set of pictures were taken from here. *27 February 1977*

BELOW: The higher elevation from Lanhydrock Road Bridge has been used for the updated picture, present-day growth and restrictions prevent standing in the precise spot, which would have been just in front of the carriage-washing plant. The common link between the two images is Prince Rock School to the top left. The former 'Up' line to the right is now the access to Friary, the former 'Down' line becoming, in 1981, the Flushing Apron for the HSTs prior to entry on to Laira Depot. There is little evidence of the Sutton Harbour Branch here. *24 June 2012.*

FRIARY JUNCTION FROM THE CATTEWATER LINE BRIDGE

We are looking back at Friary Junction and the Lanhydrock Road Bridge from the Cattewater Branch where this crossed the Sutton Harbour Branch. It is a complex area to explain in simple terms.

TOP: Plenty of interest in the top picture: to the far right behind the buildings is the direct GWR spur from Mount Gould Junction to Cattewater Junction opened on 17 January 1898 and closed on 15 September 1958. Immediately in front of the building under construction is the course of the Plymouth & Dartmoor Railway later the Lee Moor Tramway closed here in 1961, the single line of the Sutton Harbour Branch, and to the left the double track of the line from Friary Junction to Friary. *18 June 1966*

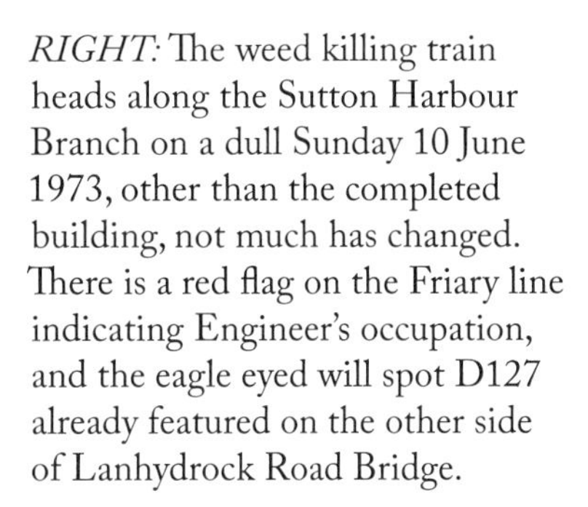

RIGHT: The weed killing train heads along the Sutton Harbour Branch on a dull Sunday 10 June 1973, other than the completed building, not much has changed. There is a red flag on the Friary line indicating Engineer's occupation, and the eagle eyed will spot D127 already featured on the other side of Lanhydrock Road Bridge.

RIGHT: A much-changed scene encountered here when visited on 23 May 2012: industrial premises have taken over the foreground completely eradicating the Sutton Harbour line at this point. It is the background houses and hills that provide the common link between the two 'Then' and the 'Now' images. Look just beyond the current builder's yard and the sharp-eyed will pick out the pylon which stands just on the Embankment Road end of Lanhydrock Road Bridge.

PRINCE ROCK THE VIEW FROM THE CATTEWATER BRANCH

ABOVE: Turning around and looking the other way from Friary Junction, this is the view from the Southern Cattewater Branch Bridge over the GWR Sutton Harbour Branch looking towards Prince Rock and the Embankment Road over bridge, which incidentally will be our next location to be visited. Beside it is the small separate bridge provided for the former Plymouth & Dartmoor Railway later the Lee Moor Tramway. 'Class 25' diesel D7573 heads down the line with the weed-killing train on Sunday 10 June 1973. It all looks neat and tidy: Stenlake Terrace is to the right, Stanley Place to the left and the Prince Rock Power Station dominates the background.

BELOW: A greatly-changed vista, as recorded on 23 May 2012, from the new cycle path which runs alongside the still extant part of the Cattewater Branch. One would hardly know the railway ran through here, although the curve of the line can still be discerned by the line of trees which have taken over much its course. The houses are still much the same and the pylon to the top left is another common feature. The greatest change is the background - the former Power Station having been demolished.

PRINCE ROCK FROM EMBANKMENT ROAD BRIDGE

ABOVE: The view looking back towards the Cattewater Branch bridge over the Sutton Harbour Branch from Embankment Road. The previous set of pictures were taken from the black bridge behind the train and the Friary Junction-Friary line can be picked out just beyond this. The course of the former Lee Moor Tramway is to the right and Stenlake Terrace is to the left. Colour pictures of the Sutton Harbour Branch are rare, and these of D7573 are the only known colour ones of a main line diesel working on the line. *10 June 1973*

BELOW: The house just above the coach in the weed-killing train in top picture is the best feature to link the two images, otherwise, yet again, growth and vegetation have over taken the view. It is hard, from this angle, to think that there was ever a railway line here. *23 May 2012*

A footnote: the perils of railway photography. On the morning D7573 ran over the Sutton Harbour Line, we had relations visiting, from Australia. I was on a three-line whip to attend the Sunday family lunch at home at 1300. Unfortunately the weed-killer ran a bit late and I turned up just as the ice cream was being served. My excuse; that is was very rare to see a main line diesel in daylight on this little-used line went down like a ton of bricks!

NORTHEYS SIDINGS

ABOVE: Just around the corner from the Embankment Road bridge, the Sutton Harbour line curved around to pass under Elliott Road Bridge by the site of Northeys sidings, which were to the rear of the train, thus just across the road from the former Western National Laira Bridge bus garage, which can be seen as the main background feature. There was a signal-box here from 1916 until 1922 when it was replaced by a Ground Frame; in layman's terms the points were unlocked by a key carried on the single line train staff. D7573 heads along the line with the 6Z07 Weed Killer *10 June 1973*

BELOW: The scene has indeed changed dramatically as many motorists will recognise this as the eastern side of Gdynia Way, the main road entrance for the City Centre from the east. Welcome to the world of the speed camera! The road from the Prince Rock direction follows the curve of the former railway line and was first constructed in the early 1980s. Northeys Sidings and, indeed, the former bus garage are long but a memory, the background hills are a good link between the two images both taken from the Elliott Road over bridge. *23 May 2012*

GDYNIA WAY FROM ELLIOTT ROAD LOOKING WEST

ABOVE: The washing is out as D7573 threads her way between Mainstone Avenue on the right, and the industrial premises on the left, beyond which is Julian Street, leading to the Cattedown Road bridge which can be seen at the far end of the cutting. The view from Elliott Road was a very rarely photographed location. *10 June 1973*

BELOW: The view is instantly still very recognisable; the road has quite simply replaced the railway. Open to debate is the drainage but that is beyond the scope of this book! Only recently has the road been widened to take two-way traffic, originally it was in-bound to the City only. I sometimes wonder how many motorists driving along there realise this was once a straight piece of railway, the Cattedown Road bridge, our next port of call, today is still a clue to the former use. *23 May 2012*

NORTH QUAY BRANCH JUNCTION

Here the Sutton Harbour line split in to two; the left-hand line going on serve Bayly's Wharf, the right-hand line serving North Quay, which we shall visit shortly.

ABOVE: A rather untidy scene as viewed from the Cattedown Road Bridge with D7573 on the Bayly's Wharf line, to the left the former premises of the Plymouth & Stonehouse Gas, Light and Coke Company and beyond lay the Commercial Road level crossing which is just beyond the wagons at the far end of the line. The railway served Lockyer's Quay, the latter a name many will recognise today with the new developments there. *10 June 1973*

BELOW: A totally unrecognisable scene today taken from exactly the same Cattedown Road over bridge vantage point. Study both pictures very carefully and for the top one go to the wagons parked up in the distance and just go to the right on the skyline. Do the same with the bottom picture and focus on the big wheel on the skyline, there just to the left of this is the Hoe War Memorial, a wonderful common link between the two images. Gdynia Way curves away to the right towards Cattedown Roundabout, almost as if taking the course of the former North Quay line. There is absolutely nothing in the present-day picture to suggest that a railway or indeed a little junction ever existed here. *23 May 2012*

ABOVE: Steam on the Sutton Harbour Branch, which is very rare in colour. The previous two images were taken from the Cattedown Road bridge, seen to the left of the rear of the train, which is standing in the siding of the former Plymouth & Stonehouse Gas, Light and Coke Company. The occasion is a Plymouth Railway Circle brake-van tour to the line hauled by 1361 Class 0-6-0 Saddle Tank no 1363. This class of only five locomotives was introduced by Churchward as a design for dock shunting in 1910. They were a very familiar sight in the Plymouth area particularly in Millbay Docks. Another use for them was coaling stage duties at Laira Shed. *3 June 1961*

RIGHT: The Cattedown Road bridge and the houses mark the spot linking the two images. Today the view is looking back up what is Gdynia Way. Possibly the correct spot would have been a little more to the left. However, even on a Sunday afternoon I thought it unwise to stand in the middle of the main road junction there! *22 September 2013*

PLYMOUTH & STONEHOUSE GAS LIGHT AND CO. SIDING

Looking the other way from the previous picture and towards the terminus of the line,1363 has now run round its brake van special and stands in the very industrial looking scene of the siding adjacent to the former Plymouth & Stonehouse Gas and Light Company Siding, a reminder of when energy was produced locally and not by foreign owned giants out to rook us for every penny possible. It all looks fairly relaxed, not a high visibility jacket in sight as the passengers take a leisurely stroll to examine the scene, and those with eagle eye sight can study the fashions of the day. Fortunately 1363 has survived and after its early days of preservation on Totnes Quay and then Bodmin Shed, it now resides at the Great Western Society base at Didcot shed, Oxfordshire. Who knows, a return visit to Plymouth one day may well be possible. *3 June 1961*

BELOW: Standing in the shadow of the Cattewater road bridge for the present day image, as can be seen there is absolutely nothing to link the two scenes other than you the reader taking my word for it. The Gas Light Company Siding is now Barbican approach, all traces of the former railway and the Gas Company have been swept away. *22 September 2013*

COMMERCIAL ROAD LEVEL CROSSING

ABOVE: The view taken outside the much recommended Thistle Park Brewhouse pub, home of the Sutton Road Brewery, where, just a few hundred yards down from the Cattewater Road bridge, the line crossed Commercial Road on a rather intricate level crossing. The line to the left is the one leading to the terminus only a very short distance away at Bayly's Wharf. The line to the right served the Sutton Harbour Goods Depot and also a cement works, but much of the traffic had by this time ceased. All lines shown here were closed by the end of 1972. It is a scene typical of the industrial railway and a backwater rarely photographed. A feature of the crossing here was the ornamental GWR inscription on the gates, which survived well in to the 1980s, and it is a pity they could not have been kept as a reminder of the previous heritage of the area. *December 1965*

BELOW: Standing again right outside the pub all evidence of the level crossing and the various sidings has been completely swept away, and the scene has changed out of all recognition. *22 September 2013*

COMMERCIAL ROAD LEVEL CROSSING

ABOVE: It is amazing what unknown information a picture can contain. Whilst showing this at a Plymouth Railway Circle meeting, member Mike Hanrahan remarked on the two cars parked on trailers on the other side of the level crossing, stating that this was a very rare image, in colour, of such vehicles. These two were 'junior stock cars' which has evolved into the present day Formula 2. Meetings were held regularly at the former Pennycross Stadium, and this being a Saturday it is more than likely these had been in use the previous night. It is probable these two vehicles were owned by a nearby scrap dealer who would thus have had easy access to spare parts. Mike informs me old timers have formed the Brisca F2 Heritage Association, and are building replicas of these cars so that stock car racing of old can return. Sadly it will not return to the long gone Pennycross Stadium. Back to railway matters and D2178 has reached the line limit at Commercial Road with the Plymouth Railway Circle Brake Van Tour. To the right of the level crossing, note the ornamental GWR insignia referred to in the previous picture, stands the rather optimistic 245 and a half mile post from Paddington via Bristol and the Weston Super Mare Avoiding line. Beyond the aforementioned stock cars, to the left can be seen the crane on Bayly's Wharf for unloading the coal brought mainly from South Wales by coastal ships, and this marked the end of the line. *18 June 1966*

LEFT: Only by locating the Civic Centre on Royal Parade seen to the right could I provide any link between the two images to show both were indeed taken from the same spot. *22 September 2013*

ST JOHN'S ROAD BRIDGE

ABOVE: We have now joined the North Quay branch and proceed to St Johns Road Bridge for the view looking back through the rather untidy cutting towards the North Quay Junction by the Cattewater Road Bridge. To the left of the engine note the point denoting the end of the loop siding from the junction. D7573 trundles down with the weed-killing train. This is the only picture I have ever seen of a train taken from here. *10 June 1973*

ABOVE: To try to give some effect to the present-day scene, I thought it best to take the updated view a few yards back from the original showing the bridge parapet and the uncontrolled forest behind which has grown up in the cutting. One would not realise today that the railway ever ran through here. *22 September 2013*

ST JOHN'S ROAD BRIDGE

ABOVE: At this time the Scrap Yard by Sutton Road was the line limit for the North Quay Branch, the track beyond here has no official closure date but was out of traffic by 1969. D7573 has arrived with its train, and the scene has a busy look about it as the scrap traffic was still healthy then. In the background there are some familiar landmarks on the city skyline with the spire of Charles Church prominent, and to its immediate left the old concrete Drake Circus car park. The rear of the NatWest Bank at the top of Royal Parade is hidden by the trees on the far left. *10 June 1973*

BELOW: You just have to take my word for it that is the same location photographed from the same spot some 39 years later. This has to be one of the most dramatic changes to be recorded in this book. Not only has any trace of the railway and the scrap yard been completely obliterated to form a new small retail park, the city skyline has changed beyond recognition, with the modern buildings and new developments. The former NatWest Bank at the top of Royal Parade is to the far left. The eagle-eyed will spot part of the sloping roof of the building on the far right, which can be picked out just above the diesel engine in the 'Then' picture. There are also a couple of houses that link the two pictures. *23 May 2012*

CROSSING SUTTON ROAD

ABOVE: To reach North Quay, the railway crossed Sutton Road on the level. The signal box here had long since been disused, the crossing being converted to hand operation circa 1914. To the right note the sign for a firm many Plymothians will remember, Isaac & Uren (Engineers) Ltd. established at Sutton Road in 1920, moving to purpose-built premises at Valley Road Plympton in June 1970. The firm did not last long in the new century going into receivership in January 2001 and being dissolved in April 2007. *October 1965*

ABOVE: Any evidence of the railway being here has been completely eradicated, but at least the wall is still recognisable. The hole in the wall denotes where the level crossing and the signal box once both existed, this is now the entrance to Travis Perkins. The Isaac & Uren hoarding has been replaced by signs for Brandon Hire, Scot Hire and Thrifty Car and Van Rental. I wonder if over time these names will one day be recalled by a future generation. *23 May 2012*

ABOVE: Just to complicate matters, the Southern had its own access to North Quay, the line descending from Friary Goods Yard through a tunnel under Exeter Street (which I presume is still there buried under all the road works and widenings), crossing Sutton Road on the level about 50 yards down the road from the GWR crossing as seen above before the two lines merged to serve the Quay. This was closed as an unnecessary duplicate in November 1951, although the track was not lifted until 1957. *October 1965*

ABOVE: There is absolutely no trace of the Southern line and its tunnel. To mark the spot I walked between the two crossings and worked from memory, and the present day shot is just about spot on. If those like myself who knew these railway lines now have difficulty in pinpointing them, one wonders how the historians of the future will manage. *23 May 2012*

NORTH QUAY

ABOVE: A picture that really captures the atmosphere of the quayside railway, where the tracks were laid amid the cobbles, and little wooden wagon turn tables connected on to further quays where only a horse or tractor would pull the wagon. Such lines were once very common but are now very much consigned to a long-past era. There is a small coastal vehicle tied up alongside; its name reads 'Antre Jansen, Uetersen.' The sole wagon, in railway terms a 'Van Fit', would not be able to go very far unless the vehicles are moved. The wagon turntable was used to shunt wagons on to Sutton Wharf which is to the right, so this was the limit of locomotive working. This was the era when North Quay was very much a place of working boats and people working in blue collar premises. *October 1965*

BELOW: The working quayside of 1965 has given way to modern buildings, high-rise and, no doubt, expensive luxury flats, the odd up-market restaurant, plenty of stone bollards on the left and, on the water, luxury pleasure craft. At least the rails survive here in the cobbles, and long may they do so because they are a reminder of the heritage of the quay. Sadly the little wooden wagon turntables have long since gone. *23 May 2012*

SUTTON WHARF

RIGHT: A picture supplied by the series editor: a view looking along Sutton Wharf toward the Cooperative warehouse and North Quay, the little wooden wagon turntable in front of the building is the same one as seen in the previous set of pictures. It is a pity that the splendid 1950s design Coop Warehouse only lasted for 40 years. The railway lines laid out in the cobbles clearly stand out in this busy industrial scene of the 1950s. How it would all soon change.

RIGHT: The view today is recognisable, just, but the hustle and bustle of the 1950s working area has given way to the high-class developments of today. The Co-operative warehouse has been replaced by the not-so-attractive Discovery Wharf, and the little wooden wagon turntable has long since vanished.

At least the rails remain as a reminder of the past industrial heritage, but here is something special. Study that piece of track on the bottom right where there is a small parallel section of rail seen by the parked car where it is bisected by the loop line on the left. Then study its course still visible in the cobbles leading up to the present Discovery Wharf Building, for that little piece of track is the only surviving section of IK Brunel's seven-foot-and-a-quarter Broad Gauge rail, in its original place, anywhere in the world. When the whole system West of Exeter was narrowed in one fell swoop over a weekend in May 1892, narrow rails were laid in to the cobbles on the quay lines here, except this one little section to save digging up the cobbles. It deserves a blue plaque. It is small, but significant and it does attract visitors - I have had many phone calls from railway enthusiasts and other interested people looking for directions to this remarkable little piece of history. I hope it can be preserved. *23 May 2012*

It is but a short walk from here up Exeter Street to the former Friary Station, where we are now heading to start the next chapter of our journey around the railways of the eastern side of Plymouth.

SUTTON HARBOUR FROM ABOVE

Through the good offices of the Plymouth Railway Circle, I have been given access to three aerial views of the city railways taken in 1957. This is looking down on North Quay and the Harbour. North Quay is to the very top left of the picture. Moving to the right, the track can be traced across Sutton Road leading to the Scrap Yard and the adjacent sidings which are well stocked with wagons. This gives some impression of the density of traffic on these little known quay lines in Plymouth. Leading down from St John's Road bridge, we come to the other part of the line with, to the right, some wagons in the actual Sutton Harbour Goods Depot. Move to the left and we see Lockyer's Quay and the terminus of the line at Bayly's Wharf, denoted by the cranes used to offload coal brought in by coastal shipping. To the left is the entrance to Sutton Harbour where, in more recent years, lock gates have been installed. Not being an angel or able to afford a helicopter, I am afraid I am unable to provide an updated picture. If one could, the changes would indeed be enormous. *27 June 1957.*

NORTH QUAY JUNCTION AND FRIARY YARD FROM ABOVE

The second of our aerial views links in well showing the close proximity of the Sutton Harbour line to the former Friary complex. Top left and the Cattedown Road over-bridge over the Sutton Harbour Branch can be identified, and, looking to the right of this, one can clearly pick out North Quay Branch Junction. Looking down towards Commercial Road level crossing, close examination of the picture reveals a Western Region 0-6-0 pannier tank engaged in shunting duties with wagons parked by the former Sutton Harbour Goods depot. Very top right the line leads to Lockyer's Quay. Returning to the Cattedown Road Bridge, a lengthy line of open wagons can be clearly seen in the long siding on the North Quay Branch, beyond them lay St John Road Bridge and the former scrap yard. Follow the road down from the Cattewater Road over-bridge and Embankment Road Methodist Church can be picked out where the present-day Cattedown Roundabout is situated. No bus lanes or traffic cameras in those days. This leads nicely in to the Tothill Road Viaduct over Friary Yard and Station, and it is to the extreme bottom right of the image we shall now move and stand to commence our examination of Friary Station with the brick-built former goods shed prominent, the yard to the left, the Locomotive Shed just beyond that and then on the former Southern lines from Friary. *27 June 1957*

PLYMOUTH FRIARY

Opened 1 July 1891 and reached from Friary Junction, this was the terminus for the London & South Western Railway, later Southern Railway, in the City. It was closed to passengers on 15 September 1958 although empty stock movements lasted another three years. The Station became the main goods station for Plymouth under the BR Modernisation Plan but, as traffic dwindled away, total closure was inevitable and the short-lived freight concentration depot had gone by 1987. These three pictures are taken from the northern end of the Tothill Road Viaduct, which was originally constructed to cross the whole complex. Now, sadly, no rails pass beneath it. Look out in particular, in all three pictures, for three common landmarks: to the right the spire of Charles Church, to its left the Civic Centre in Royal Parade and just to the left of that, the tower of St Andrews Church.

LEFT: A general view of the terminus in October 1965 looking towards the buffer stops when it was all still intact. The station was, like the adjacent St Judes Church, the aforementioned Tothill Road Viaduct and many of nearby houses, built of light-grey limestone. It did not have the hustle and bustle of its nearby GWR neighbours North Road and Millbay, but had a sort of tranquillity of its own. To the right a goods platform, then the bay once used by Turnchapel trains. The main platforms were separated by a third line mainly for locomotive release purposes. To the left stands the former Friary 'B' Signal Box closed on 21 July 1962 next to the substantial goods shed. A compact little terminal ideal for railway modelling.

LEFT: One of the last locomotives to be seen in the old station, 37 196 runs around its weed-killing train on 26 April 1987. The station buildings and platform awnings were demolished in 1976, and the goods shed replaced by the short lived Freight Concentration Depot which at this time was about to close. The track layout had been altered but the scene was still recognisable.

LEFT: Friary Station has now vanished and been replaced by retail units, one could be forgiven for not knowing the station had ever existed here. The three main landmarks remain in the back ground. *6 November 2011*

PLYMOUTH FRIARY, FURTHER MEMORIES

Three further views of Friary from the south end of the Tothill Road Viaduct.

TOP: The former goods shed was a substantial red-brick building, and even in 1965, some 18 years after the demise of the Southern Railway, the SR notice proudly advised that its entrance was in Exeter Street. The Shed was demolished not long after this picture was taken to make way for the new Freight Concentration Depot. *October 1965*

MIDDLE: The replacement Friary Freight Concentration Depot opened on 20 June 1966 with a staff of about 120. Political interference with how the Railway handled its parcels traffic led, in the early 1970s, of the creation of National Carriers, one of whose large road trailers can be seen parked up outside the depot. Inevitably the parcels traffic went more and more by road. Talking of road vehicles, here is something different, the delivery of the first passenger coach to the Plym Valley Railway. Since the PVR has no physical connection with the national system, everything must come in by road. In our early days, we purchased a Brake Second Coach, and loan of the former Laira Breakdown vehicle. These were taken off their rail bogies in Friary Yard before being placed on a special road bogie for the short run over to the PVR base at Marsh Mills. *15 September 1983.*

BOTTOM: The very sad scene only six and a half years later as Friary is razed to the ground. The Freight traffic had finished in 1987, returning to Tavistock Junction Yard and the railway pulled out and sold off the land. .
March 1990

HOW TO BRING EXETER STREET TO A GRINDING HALT

BELOW: The coach bound for the Plym Valley Railway reversed out of Friary Yard with a very skillful piece of driving by the haulier. Just before the coach moved, a member of the haulier's staff ran in to Exeter Street to block off the traffic for the few moments this move would take. I do not recall even a police presence let alone an escort. Common sense prevailed and the job was done with minimal interference. On that day, a lady stood at the bus stop asked me what all the fuss was about. I simply replied *'there is a train coming.'*

RIGHT: Job done, coach reversed into Exeter Street, all done without any hassle in a couple of minutes.

LEFT: The lady at the bus stop looks on somewhat bemused at the none-too-common sight of a railway coach heading towards the Cattedown Roundabout; no hold ups, no escort. Note the man riding at the very rear of the vehicle controlling the braking and the steering.

RIGHT: Since the coach was not travelling very fast, I thought a shot somewhere en route would be a possibility. I headed up to Military Road as this gave a higher elevation to view the spectacle, and with perfect timing the 0930 from Paddington went the other way on the main line. One of those golden moments, the unplanned shot, road and rail at Laira! *15 September 1982*

FRIARY YARD

ABOVE: We return to the northern end of the Tothill Road Viaduct, this time looking east, the passenger station directly behind the photographer on the other side of the road. Friary Yard was quite spacious and, when in use as part of the Freight Concentration Scheme, could be quite busy. There is a long line of freight wagons in the siding and plenty of National Carriers trailers are parked up. On what used to be the main running-line into the passenger station, 'Western' Class D1048 'Western Lady' has called in with 6V53 0313 Etruria to St Blazey. This was the clay empties returning home from the Potteries. The train was also used to convey general freight forward from Exeter Riverside Yard; thus the need to run via Friary. The link to North Quay started on the far right, but the tunnel from the Yard had long since been filled in at this end. Desborough Road is behind, Knighton Road to the left. *6 September 1976*

BELOW: The much-changed and rather depressing scene of today. Friary is no longer used for freight or any other traffic. The former main line is, in effect, just a run round point for what is now a very under used branch from Friary Junction to the remains of the Cattewater Branch; the odd enthusiast special may put in an appearance now and again. The Yard is desolate and will become yet another housing development in the near future, so this scene is likely to change. 37 259 front and 37 604 rear with 1Q13 Network Rail Radio Test Train pause as they reverse on their way back from the Cattewater line. *3 May 2012*

FRIARY YARD

We now move to the south end of the Tothill Road Viaduct for three more views of Friary Yard to reflect the changing scene. Desborough Road is to the right, Knighton Road to the left.

LEFT: The rather spacious Yard in 1965 when preparations were under way for the Freight Concentration Depot; some goods traffic can be seen. In the background Friary 'A' signal box can be spotted along with the signals which controlled the junction with the Cattewater Junction line and the shed entrance. This signal box closed on 24 April 1966.

LEFT: It all still looks neat and tidy as Class 33 diesels 33 106 leading and 33 104 on the rear haul Bournemouth Line TC sets, very rare in this part of the world let alone Friary, call in on the way home from Carne Point via Bere Alston with 1Z21 Rail Tour on its way back to London Waterloo. The basic layout is the same, plenty of china clay wagons, probably from Marsh Mills, to the right one of the Plymstock cement wagons. *16 April 1977*

LEFT: Just three tracks remain, mainly for running around purposes, as reversal is necessary to reach the remaining stub of the Cattewater Branch. In charge of the Network Rail Radio test train 37 259 front and 37 604 rear pause to reverse towards Laira and the main line. The vegetation on the Knighton Road side of the yard has taken a firm grip. Housing development may well alter the scene in the near future. *3 May 2012*

FRIARY YARD FROM DESBOROUGH ROAD

BELOW: As already mentioned, Friary became the principal freight depot for the City in 1966. This was to last barely 20 years as the role went back to Tavistock Junction in 1987, one of the reasons being residents' objections to having a 24-hour freight yard and the attendant shunting going on 24 hours a day. There is not much traffic in the yard, possibly due to this being a Saturday, but note how well laid out it is, and how neat and tidy everything appears. In the foreground the nearest line marks the spot where the line through the tunnel to North Quay commenced. This filled in to give further space to the Yard. Tothill Road Viaduct is to the left, behind the train is St Judes Church and Knighton Road is to the right. A Class 31 diesel on the weed-killer awaits the next move. *April 1984.*

RIGHT: There is but one very short gap in the present-day fencing here to point the camera and update the somewhat now depressing scene. Only the three tracks on the Knighton Road side remain, and this is only really for any, now very rare, train proceeding to the remains of the Cattewater Branch to reverse, or to host the odd enthusiast rail tour, which appear now and again. The rest of the yard was lifted after the cessation of freight traffic, and is now the subject of a planning application for housing, so this scene is likely to change in the future. *22 September 2013.*

FROM TOTHILL PARK

ABOVE: The rebuilt Bulleid Pacifics were not seen in the City until 1960 when the restriction on them crossing Meldon Viaduct near Okehampton was lifted. They soon became a regular sight, but only for four short years, the era of regular Southern steam ending with the withdrawal of the through trains from Waterloo via Okehampton (except for the down overnight which lasted until March 1967). One regular performer was 34096 'Trevone,' seen here in glorious evening sunshine pulling away from Friary, with the former Lucas Terrace Halt behind, with the empty coaching stock for the 1918 Plymouth-Exeter Central via Okehampton known as 'The Mail'. I last saw this engine on 29 August 1964 when photographing it at Meldon Junction on the 1652 Plymouth - Eastleigh (another wonderful train which lasted until March 1967 and one could have spent 11 hours on it travelling to Waterloo, arriving at 0343). When 'Trevone' reached Exmouth Junction shed after the working that train that particular evening, the fire was dropped and the locomotive withdrawn from traffic. Nothing wrong with it, just a case of no more work for it to do. Yet another example of the head-long rush for dieselisation casting aside fine locomotives like 'Trevone' which surely would have had many more years of work left in them. *June 1961*

BELOW: Despite all the many changes, it was not too hard to identify the correct location for the present-day image, this being the only piece of raised ground in Tothill Park adjacent to the railway, just behind the Tothill Community Centre and Library. Also note the position and levels of the tracks which confirm the location. 'Trevone' was on the nearest track which drops down the short distance to Friary Junction, and the remaining stub of the Cattewater Branch by Lucas Terrace Halt behind. The allotments have long since gone, Tothill Community Centre and Library taking over the foreground, and the new housing on the site of Friary Shed has transformed the background. *22 September 2013*

FRIARY SHED

ABOVE: The entrance to the shed was just by the junction between the main line to Friary Junction and the Branch to Cattewater Junction. Going back to 1956 in a scene that would have remained unchanged for decades, one of the long-standing Southern Plymouth area locomotives Class 'O2' 30192 stands at the Shed entrance, the houses in Lanhydrock Road to the left a good reference point. The O2s were at this time mainly employed on Callington Branch duties with some local workings also to Tavistock, and Devonport King's Road shunt engine including trips to Stonehouse Pool. *July 1956*

BELOW: Friary Shed and its approach and sidings have all been swept away under recent housing developments and there is no trace of anything to be found. Thus updating pictures does present a challenge to find some marker, or a reference point or any common link. Standing in what is now Junction Gardens, the wooded hill on the far right provides the required link between the two images. *4 September 2013*

FRIARY SHED

ABOVE: History has failed to record a precise opening date for Friary Shed, but as far as I can ascertain the London & South Western Railway brought it in to use in 1898. This was a much smaller shed than Laira, consisting of one three-road shed with a hoist alongside, a small yard at each end, and a not particularly large coaling stage. It passed to the control of the Western Region in February 1958 and closed in May 1963 and demolished the following year. There is no trace whatsoever of the facility today. Under the British Railways Shed Code Numbering system introduced in May 1950, and based on the former London Midland & Scottish Railway format, Friary became 72D as part of the sheds in the Exmouth Junction Division. On passing to the Western Region in February 1958 it became 83H, taking the next available slot in what was the Newton Abbot Division. In a scene that probably never altered over the decades and one I certainly remember, 'O2' 30236 allocated to Friary from August 1950 to December 1955 stands outside the western end of the shed with the hoist alongside on the right. *16 November 1952*

ABOVE: I can offer little comment on the present-day view taken only from memory, but I assure you it is not too far out. *4 September 2013*

FRIARY SHED

There is a very tenuous link between the two images here and it is the Lanhydrock Road bridge, which we have already visited in our look at Mount Gould, Friary Junction and the Sutton Harbour Branch. This can be spotted to the far right in the top picture. Very careful examination of the bottom picture on the left in the gap between the two trees, the bend on the Mount Gould side on the end of Lanhydrock Road Bridge can just be picked out. This took a lot of working out due to the palisade fencing and the runaway growth, I was only able to point my camera to just get this in on the left, ideally it should be a bit more to the right but I think you can get the general drift.

ABOVE: Just before closure of the shed, 'Ivatt' Tank 41206 at rest on Friary Depot. I remember years ago when entertaining one of the local enthusiasts at home, a great friend ours the late Geoffrey Salmon, who came originally from Yorkshire, on seeing this picture remarked that, on the day of Nationalisation, this was a Hellifield allocated engine. On checking the records he was of course correct. The 2-6-2 LMS-designed Ivatt Tanks proved to be a very successful successor to the O2s and the M7s in the West Country, and by the time this picture was taken 41206 was an Exmouth Junction engine. *March 1963*

RIGHT: Not a lot to enthuse over in the updated scene. *4 September 2013*

FRIARY SHED – SOME FURTHER MEMORIES

RIGHT: An undated 1950s view of 'M7' 30035 at rest outside the Shed. In my childhood days, 30034,30035 and 30036 were the stalwarts of the local services to and from Tavistock North, and a train I fondly recall only ever being 'M7' hauled was the 1614 Plymouth to Brentor. This trio were all allocated to Friary throughout the 1950s.

RIGHT: A spring 1962 look at another of the trio, 30034 in the evening sunshine with the coaling stage behind. Timeless.

RIGHT: Another spring 1962 shot,and just to remind or inform those unaware of how photography has changed in recent years with the advent of the digital format, the slide scanner and Photoshop. This picture of another Friary stalwart, allocated here April 1954 to March 1962, 'O2' 30225; another one I recall from my early days. The picture was taken on a Voightlander, not even a single lens reflex, with, I think, 25 ASA Kodachrome film. I held the oil drum steady so Mr Hocking could take the half-a-second frame, and we were really chuffed it came out. The quality was not what one would expect nowadays and only by now being able to scan the original in, and then work on it for a considerable period of time can you end up with this respectable digital image. One of the few interior shots of Friary Shed I have ever seen, and yes it really does capture the atmosphere. Soot, smoke, grime and an aura all of its own. Wonderful!

LUCAS TERRACE HALT

This was the first station out of Friary on the line to Cattewater Junction. Served by Turnchapel trains, it was 120 feet long and seven feet wide, originally of timber construction and opened in October 1905 and closed 10 September 1951. From 3 November 1941 to 7 October 1947 it was also served by the GWR service to and from Yealmpton. The view is looking west towards Friary.

ABOVE: A splendid view taken by Mr Ken Holdaway, a former President of the Plymouth Railway Circle, of an 'Up' express more than likely the 1135 Friary to London Waterloo shortly after commencing its journey. The view is from Lucas Terrace Halt on which the photographer is standing. The express, with a Class 'N,' is on the double track to Friary Junction. On the left just off the platform is Friary Shed which we have just visited, and a fine array of signals protecting the branch at its Junction controlled from the former Friary 'A' Signal Box. Note also the delightful little waiting shelter on the Halt, a typical Exmouth Junction (Exeter) Concrete Works specimen. *Summer 1958*

BELOW: A quarter of a century later, there is much to link the two pictures as the view is broadly similar. Tothill Park and Playing Fields on the right look much the same, the Cattewater Line has gained a new quarter mile post from its junction outside Friary Yard. In the background the Civic Centre has risen up in the distance on Royal Parade. Lucas Terrace Halt shows signs of decay as the little waiting shelter has long since been demolished. To the left, Friary Shed has been demolished and at the time had become a fertiliser depot. A Class 31 diesel heads for Friary Junction with the weed-killing train. The scene would see further changes as we shall see in the next set of pictures. *May 1984*

LUCAS TERRACE HALT

We continue our journey through the years here looking west from Lucas Terrace Halt.

TOP: Rare visitors to the Cattewater Line in respect of the then 'Hunslet Barclay' (who at time had the contract for running the weed-killing trains) owned former BR Class 20s renumbered as 20 904 seen here leading and 20 901 on the rear, approaching Lucas Terrace Halt. The Fertiliser Depot on the site of the former Friary Shed was at this time still served by rail, the traffic coming by train 6V35 1728 (Sundays) Ince and Elton to Truro which dropped off a portion at Exeter St Davids for Lapford (on the Exeter--Barnstaple Branch), then running direct to Friary reversing there for the onward journey to Cornwall departing at 0328 Monday morning, which probably explains why none of the local railway enthusiasts ever photographed it! *8 April 1990*

MIDDLE: There is an air of dereliction setting in as the new century takes hold. The view point is slightly different as Lucas Terrace Halt had been demolished due to the impending construction of the new cycle path and growth is starting to obscure the view of the park on the right. The green coaches add to the memories of the former Southern trains, which once ran through here, as 66 199 heads probably the longest train seen here in many a year with 1Z42 Rail Tour from Finsbury Park to Carne Point (Fowey). *1 July 2000*

BOTTOM: The present-day view with substantial fencing to protect the cycle path provides an obstacle to any photography of the railway here. The Fertiliser Depot which was on the site of Friary Shed has been obliterated by the recent housing development of the site. *23 May 2012.*

LUCAS TERRACE HALT

ABOVE: In railway photography terms, this is what I would describe as a nice little branch-line shot. It is certainly a very rare one as the number of appearances of Class 20s on the Cattewater Branch can be counted on the fingers of one hand. Despite being just outside Friary and very close to the City Centre, the picture has an almost rural look about it with the trees on the left behind the line to Friary Junction sheltering the view of Tothill Park and Mount Gould. The full length of Lucas Terrace Halt and its situation on a slight curve shows up very well. Behind the train the line can be seen curving away towards Cattewater Junction. 20 901 leads the weed-killing train back through the grass-grown platform towards Friary on a lovely spring afternoon. *8 April 1990*

BELOW: There is certainly no rural look about the scene today. The blue signpost is at the top of the steps where one accessed the former little station from the road below and the line of the fence does follow the same curve as the former platform. The railway lines are still there to the left of the fence, the cycle path at this point running parallel to the tracks. A scene that has not changed for the better. *23 May 2012*

LUCAS TERRACE HALT

ABOVE: A rather personal little memory here as this was the first Rail Tour I ever travelled on as a very young 14 year old lad. The occasion was the running of the last train to convey passengers from Plymouth Friary to Turnchapel; a goods brake van special organised by the Plymouth Railway Circle, the start of a long and very happy association with this Society which is still going strong. Thus this is my first photographic stop with any train, we all piled out at Lucas Terrace Halt and as far as I know, this was the last train to ever call there. The motive power was Class 'M7' 30034, one of the Plymouth trio already mentioned whilst discussing Friary Shed. This class of locomotive were not normally seen on Turnchapel Branch trains, so we do have a rare visitor to the line. To the right the double track of the main line curves away to Friary Junction, the spire of St Jude's Church in the far background provides a local landmark. *30 September 1961*

BELOW: Using my little portable step-ladder, I was just able to get high enough above the present day fence to record the much-changed scene, using the curve of the former main line round to Friary Junction as the common link between the two images, and careful study of the bushes will reveal the spire of St. Judes Church. *23 May 2012.*

LUCAS TERRACE HALT

The view looking east towards Friary Junction to the left and Cattewater Junction to the right.

LEFT: After its exploits down the Sutton Harbour Branch, D7573 rounds the curve from Friary Junction towards the former Friary Station with the weed killer. On the left Tothill Park, far left background Lanhydrock Road bridge, which we have now discussed more than once. I am standing on Lucas Terrace Halt with the single line leading away to Cattewater Junction, with, on the far right, the black bridge that took the Southern Cattewater Branch over the GWR Sutton Harbour Branch. We have already examined the view each way from this structure. A complicated area which I hope I have been able to explain clearly in simple terms. *10 June 1973*

LEFT: By the dawn of the new Century changes are evident. Friary Junction-Friary was singled retaining the former 'Up' line. The former 'Down' line was adapted to become the site for the Flushing Apron, now regarded as part of Laira Depot. The changes took effect as from 11 February 1980. A little piece of history here as 67 010 and 67 014 round the curve with 1Z42 0743 Finsbury Park (London)-Carne Point (Fowey) via Friary, as we have already seen 66 199 was attached to the rear after the Friary reversal. This was the first scheduled passenger working for this recently introduced Class of locomotive. The scene is still recognisable despite some growth, larger trees in particular. *1 July 2000*

LEFT: Plenty of vegetation nowadays to spoil the view, the angle at a slightly higher elevation due to growth and the cycle-path fence. *23 May 2012*

APPROACHING CATTEWATER JUNCTION

ABOVE: We have now gone over the Sutton Harbour Line on the black bridge seen in the picture at the top of the previous page, and also crossed Embankment Road and are now dropping down to Cattewater Junction where the lines to the Cattewater and over the iron bridge to Plymstock split. Picture is taken from the Plymouth Railway Circle Plymouth Area Brake Van tour hauled by Class 03 D2178. Note the allotments in the foreground, and to the right Prince Rock School Playing Fields, the running-track can be clearly picked out with on the left by the bend, the long and high-jump pits, the latter is the white one facing the railway line. The Nissen hut in the right background was the school canteen, the school children being marched down and back each lunchtime and it is from here we will look back for the present-day view. My chances of a precise update from a brake-van special, it must be admitted, are few. *18 June 1966.*

BELOW: With the construction of the new relief road from Embankment Road for traffic to Plymstock, a new photographic location became available, and was put to good use when 37 604 and 37 259 visited the line with the Network Rail Radio Test train, the first train as far as I know in about four and a half years to run down here, so little is the line used today. The view is looking back from Cattewater Junction towards the curve seen above, and I am standing where the Nissen hut dining-room as seen above was located. Finding a new photographic location on the Cattewater Branch in 2012 I thought was a remarkable achievement. One can only wonder how long it will be before the vegetation takes over and blocks this rather excellent view point. *3 May 2012*

CATTEWATER JUNCTION

A favourite photographic location and a very accessible one is the view of Cattewater Junction right on the city end of the Laira Road Bridge, and here is a series of four photographs with an assortment of motive power over the years to show the changes as they evolved.

ABOVE: The way things were as 31 424 on the front and 37 299 on the rear have charge of the annual weed-killing train; plenty of history to discuss here. One quite remarkable survivor is alongside the leading locomotive, the level crossing gate marking where the former Plymouth & Dartmoor, later the Lee Moor Tramway horse-worked line crossed the LSWR Cattewater Branch. To the right is the line over the River Plym to Plymstock. Behind the train a fairly new building has been constructed for 'Barbican' on the Dartmoor Line formation, and Laira Bridge bus garage is just visible on the extreme left. 1 *May 1982*

BELOW: Moving on by eight years as 20 904 leading and 20 901 on the rear provide the first known visit of Class 20 diesels to the line, there are some subtle changes. The main one is the line over the river to Plymstock that was by now closed to all traffic and quietly rusting away. Just as well as I do not think the straying dogs would have been any match for a train. The Dartmoor Line Level Crossing Gate is still there, but the blue building has lost its 'Barbican' sign. In the far background, where the line crosses Embankment Road, the bridge has had a repaint and the blue rather stands out. Otherwise the very attractive view remained much the same. *8 April 1990*

ABOVE: As the scene here passes in to the new century, there are some notable changes and a very rare visitor to the line in the form of a single car first generation DMU, known affectionately as 'Bubble Cars', this one taken into departmental use and fitted with a camera to record every section of track on the system, as can be clearly seen. The former 55025 renumbered as 960011 is going about this duty as it trundles along the line running as 2Z02 0630 St Blazey to Tavistock Junction. Looking a bit battered and bruised, the level-crossing gate for the Dartmoor line is still there, just. To the right, the former Plymstock line leading to the Laira rail bridge has become a cycle path, the blue building behind the train is now for 'Pirtek', and over on the left, the former Western National Laira Bridge bus garage has been demolished. *28 March 2001*

BELOW: Bringing the story right up to date, much has indeed changed. The former Plymstock line on the right, now a cycle path, is completely hidden by vegetation. The level crossing gate for the Dartmoor line has finally been laid to rest, the blue building and the Nissen hut have been swept away to make room for the new relief road from Embankment Road towards Plymstock. One common feature, the pylon on the extreme left, is ever-present in all four pictures, as is the footbridge which has become more visible over the years. 37 259, leading with 37 604 at the rear, approaches the former Cattewater Junction very slowly with the Network Rail Radio Test Train. *3 May 2012*

CATTEWATER BRANCH, LAIRA WHARVES

ABOVE: Crossing the road (much easier for the 'Then' picture) from the Cattewater Junction shot to the western side of the Laira Road Bridge, a scene that had probably changed little over the years. A Branch Line Society Plymouth-area rail tour formed of a three-car DMU passes by. On the extreme bottom left of the picture, there are traces to be seen of the Dartmoor Gauge four-foot six-inch rails, this line ran as far as this Wharf. The buildings are no doubt of some antiquity, and were at the time looking a bit worse for wear.. *10 October 1970*

BELOW: The actual railway track and the rock face to the right are all that remain, otherwise everything else has been swept away to make way for the modern-day boat marina. 37 604 brings up the rear of the Network Rail Radio Test Train. How many more trains we shall ever see here is a matter of debate. *3 May 2012*

LAIRA WHARVES

Moving along Laira Bridge a few yards to the left, a selection of broader views to show how Laira Wharves changed over the years.

ABOVE: The scrap-yard looks busy with a once-proud submarine being cut up. The Dartmoor Gauge track has finally gone, but the old Wharf buildings are still there. An on the whole rather untidy looking scene as 37 299 leads 31 424 with the weed-killer. *1 May 1982*

ABOVE: The scene is indeed changing as the old buildings are being demolished. 20 901 leading with 20 904 on the rear with the weed-killer hard at work! *8 April 1990*

ABOVE: All the history and the old buildings have been swept away to make way for a marina. The former 55025 is now filming the track in the other direction as the train heads back towards Friary. No trace of the wharf buildings remain. *28 March 2001*

ABOVE: The present day scene with the Network Rail Radio Test Train having gone as far as it can on the branch. Just beyond the train a large iron gate protects the scrap yard and as we see shortly, just beyond there is the end of the line. The branch has been retained to this point for any potential traffic from the scrap yard, but this seems unlikely at present. Scrap is still loaded from St Blazey and Alphington Road, Exeter (on the remaining stub of the former Teign Valley Branch) to Alexandra Dock Junction, Newport South Wales, whether we shall this traffic from here again, who knows? It would secure the future of the last remaining line of the once numerous railways that served various quays in the city. *3 May 2012*

CASTLE'S SHIPBREAKING CO. LTD.

BELOW: A splendid view from a slide given to me by my old friend Brian Gibson showing a three-car DMU rail tour heading past the scrap-yard and approaching Corporation Wharf. This is where the coal brought in by Colliers from South Wales for the Power Station was unloaded. Undated, but almost certainly an early 1980s image, this clearly reflects the Industrial nature of the area served by this line, and just how close some of the different wharves and sidings were to each other. The River Plym shows up well in this picture. On the left on the opposite bank is the village of Turnchapel with Staddon Heights to the right dominating the background. *Circa 1980*

BELOW: The area has changed so much in recent years it is hard to get one's bearings at times and I could not find any trace of the original viewpoint. Today this is the end of the line, the Branch being truncated back to this point when the remainder of the line was lifted late 2009/early 2010. The buffer stop is situated more or less just ahead of the tank wagons seen in the original picture to the right in the British Glues & Chemicals Siding. *24 June 2012.*

PETHICK'S QUAY

Although the Cattewater Branch was a very short line of only a couple of miles - it served a considerable number of industrial locations with a multitude of sidings - one can get confused when the latter overran into each other. To complicate matters some of the businesses changed names or moved out to make way for a new name which may well have seen an industrial change of use of the site. This set of pictures was taken about a quarter of a mile or so further on from the scrap yard views on the proceeding page.

RIGHT: One of the classic photographic locations on the line was the river wall here at Pethick's Quay. Looking east 37 196 is seen with the annual weed-killing train. The line was in the main worked by the smaller diesel shunting engines, and usually early in the morning making photography difficult. The yearly weed killer which brought main line diesels to the branch normally ran at a weekend in the spring and at a time more favourable to obtain decent pictures of the branch. *May 1987*

RIGHT: I could not really make up my mind whether to include the Class 37 picture, or the Class 20 as both are powerful images of the train in the industrial setting. So I have compromised and included both! Enjoy this one of 20 904. In both images Corporation Wharf is in the background to the rear of the train, and to the left is the Blight & White factory. *8 April 1990*

RIGHT: When I came to update these pictures, I got a little confused as I had not realised there had been substantial land reclamation here and found out the hard way. The course of the line was now about 500 yards at least from the river. Working on the background hills and pacing around with prints of the originals in my hand, this is spot on. It is hard to believe this is the same location. *24 June 2012*

PASSAGE HOUSE INN CROSSING

ABOVE: Crossing to the other side of the line and turning round to look west, we reach the Passage House Inn level crossing. The gates can be spotted to the right on the curve just beyond the train. This is another typical industrial setting which reflects the character of the line as the Branch Line Society Rail Tour pauses for a photographic stop. The building just behind the train is still with us and will feature in further coverage of this now much changed scene. Just beyond the latter it is interesting to note some goods vans parked in Passage House Inn Siding. Due to the great changes in the area, this is another location where a precise update is very difficult, so we will cross to the other side of the track. *10 October 1970*

BELOW LEFT: Standing more or less in the middle of where the train is situated in the above picture, a Class 31 Diesel waits to cross the road. Passage House Inn Siding, referred to above, is quietly rusting away to the left. The building has become 'Wellington Welding Supplies and an oil storage tank has been constructed. Note my little 100E car 'Western Empire' which took me thousands of miles in the noble pursuit of railway photography. *April 1964*

BOTTOM RIGHT: Whilst looking the other way at the former Pethick's Wharf, surprisingly I noticed this angle did have some common reference points. The course of the line just inside the fence is one, 'Wellington Welding Supplies' are still there with a new sign, and the oil storage tank has changed colour. No trace remains of the former Passage House Inn Siding. *24 June 2012*

PASSAGE HOUSE INN CROSSING

ABOVE: A real blast from the past recalling the days when the area was served by Plymouth City Transport in the form of circular service 3A Cattedown-Peverell-Milehouse-Devonport -City Centre-Cattedown and 4A which ran in the other direction. This was of course the era of Plymouth Joint Services when Western National also ran a service 22 West Hoe-Breton Side-Cattedown, the timetable going to great pains to inform one that the 22 stopped *outside* Breton Side Bus Station. Like the railways, the buses have seen great changes and, similar to the railway, not for the better. The Leyland PD2s had served Plymouth for many years, but the end of the traditional double-decker with front half cab and stairs at the back, as well as a friendly conductor were fast disappearing as the change to one-man operated vehicles got under way. The batch OCO 500-520 fleet numbers 100-120, the latter displayed in gold leaf and clearly visible here, were the last Leyland traditional buses built for Plymouth City Transport and introduced in 1958. In February 1974 the then Plymouth Bus Club ran a farewell tour covering many of their former routes, and OCO 520 pauses for the camera whilst crossing the Cattewater branch. I was, incidentally, instrumental in the preservation of OCO 502. Behind are the premises of Castle Kitchens who subsequently relocated to Estover. *February 1974*

ABOVE: The area has changed so much it is difficult to realise there was even a railway level crossing here. The present-day road is known as Shapters Way and the track bed is discernible either side of the former level crossing. *24 June 2012*

PASSAGE HOUSE INN CROSSING

ABOVE: Standing on the level crossing looking through the rather well-worn gates back towards Pethick's Quay, 31 231 waits patiently for permission to proceed. There are already signs of that dreaded word 'rationalisation' which seemed to creep into railway vocabulary from the late 1960s as the left-hand line was partially lifted after being taken out of use on 20 May 1979. Judging by the amount of weeds and flowers on the running track, there is plenty of work for 31 231 and its weed-killer to do! *April 1984*

MIDDLE: It looks as if the weed killing was successful as there is a more tidy look to the rails as 37 196 waits to cross the road. To the left are the substantial premises of Blight & White. *26 April 1987*

BOTTOM: The present day scene speaks for itself as the track bed can still be discerned here and the industrial buildings of Blight & White to the left remain in position to provide a link between the two images of when trains used to wait to cross the road here. *24 June 2012.*

PASSAGE HOUSE INN CROSSING

BELOW: This location was known locally for many years as Hocking's Crossing, the reason for which is fairly obvious as the building now used by Wellington Welding Supplies, was formerly the business of Hocking Brothers. They dealt with things maritime, and, amongst other things, they used to store in the winter and maintain the rafts which were positioned in the summer months on the east side of the Lido at Tinside for the enjoyment of swimmers taking a dip in that part of the Sound. We are looking east over the level crossing, and a delightful little scene as Class 03 Diesel Shunter D2178 runs around the Plymouth Railway Circle Plymouth Area Brake Van Tour, Hocking Brothers are to the right and participants on the Special look on with not an orange jacket in sight. *18 June 1966*

BOTTOM: The curve of the line from the level crossing towards the photographer is very evident in this updated view and is a good link between the two images. To the right, Hocking Brothers have long since gone and Wellington Welding Supplies now occupy the site. *24 June 2012*

CATTEWATER TUNNEL

ABOVE: The principal engineering feature of the line was the 48-yard Cattewater Tunnel, as here the line made a short deviation inland from the river bank and the many quays. The tunnel precluded the passage of larger engines along the branch, and indeed due to its narrow construction some types of rolling stock. 37 196 has gone as far as it can, the class being barred from passing through the tunnel. The view is from Passage House Inn Crossing looking west, Hocking Brothers and Wellington Welding Supplies are behind the photographer. *26 April 1987*

ABOVE: The oil tank has changed colour and a few more trees have grown up above the tunnel mouth, but overall the two images are comparable. *24 June 2012*

THE VIEW FROM BREAKWATER HILL LOOKING EAST

ABOVE: A very industrial scene looking down on South West Tar Distillers Works, and the sheer number of wagons parked up in the various sidings give a good impression of how busy the railway was serving this plant. The bitumen came from Fawley Refinery, near Southampton, normally on train 6V62 which ran at least three days most weeks. As far as I know, the traffic ended as the bitumen wagons were life-expired, and in the un-joined up world of the now privatised railway there was little appetite from anybody to invest in a new fleet of wagons and the traffic finished in April 2008. Notice on the left in the yard, under the cliff, an avalanche shelter has been constructed to protect workers and equipment from falling rocks. On the other side of the river we are looking towards Turnchapel Village and Staddon Heights. *July 1982*

ABOVE: The scene is still recognisable today. The bitumen wagons are of course no more, but careful examination reveals some of the tracks they stood on are still there embedded in the ground. The avalanche shelter on the left is another feature that has remained in place, the concrete bridge to the right has vanished. Possibly the biggest changes are in the background on the other side of the River Plym where Turnchapel has really altered with the marina and its sea of masts. *4 September 2013*

THE VIEW FROM BREAKWATER HILL LOOKING WEST

ABOVE: A splendid panorama looking west on what is an industrial scene with some local landmarks in the background which help one gain some bearing on the area. To the extreme left is the Civic Centre on Royal Parade with the tower of St Andrew's Church just to its right. In the middle of the picture just above the bitumen wagons, the spire of Charles Church is visible. We are looking down on Plymouth Tar Works which not that long before existed on both sides of the railway line; the south side being demolished to make way for the Conoco Oil Distribution tanks which tend to dominate the picture. *July 1982*.

BELOW: Much has changed in the intervening years, and it did not help when working out the updated picture that the Conoco Oil Distribution Tanks have changed appearance and reduced in numbers. There is little evidence that the railway ran through here and the former Tar Works are but a memory, although our landmarks - the Civic Centre, St Andrew's tower and Charles Church spire - are useful reference points. *4 September 2013*

WESTERN FUELS LTD., ORIGINALLY WESTCOTT COAL SIDING

For a line of such a short length, it is surprising just how many wharfs and sidings existed to serve the various factories, tar works, oil distribution depots, etc. As we almost reach journeys end, we call in at Western Fuels where yet again the railway served industry.

ABOVE: Western Fuels looking west towards the branch terminus. The line was still in use here as modern wagons are parked up on the left awaiting clay traffic. This was a short lived contract with Victoria Wharf. To the right the entrance to the former Anglo-American Oil Company (later to become Esso), Fuel Depot was unique, an arch being cut through the cliff face to reach the 'Deadman's Bay' Quarry Depot (the name referencing the loss of several ships and many men there, notably in the storm of 1827). To the left again, one can just spot the top of the former 'Bird Cage' siding, so named because of netting on the rock face. In the early days of the Plym Valley Railway, in the 1980s, we stored some redundant ex-Devonport Dockyard wagons here before their transfer to our site at Marsh Mills. *3 September 1991*

UPPER RIGHT: The same place location looking the other way, east, a quiet industrial back water scene, yet there is plenty of interest. The line into the fuel terminal through the rock face is the one leading off to the left. Note the one-and-three-quarter mile-post from Friary, and yet more oil storage tanks, and the line is still in use with wagons stabled. *3 September 1991*

LOWER RIGHT: It is totally impossible to obtain any form of picture update here today as the whole area is surrounded by high unfriendly fencing. Through the good offices of my friends at Victoria Wharf, I was able to poke my camera through the fence and obtain the present day view, about 50 yards or so further distant than the middle view. The expected vegetation hinders the updated scene but look to the background of this and the middle view, the distant houses and Staddon Heights are good reference points. The right-hand oil storage tanks are still there, but hidden by the vegetation. *4 September 2013*

VICTORIA WHARVES

ABOVE: The final destination of the Cattewater Branch was Victoria Wharves, which were for a many years owned by Coast Lines. By 1977 the owner's name had changed to Bethell Gwyn and Co. In 1991 I have it recorded as Escombe Lambert Ltd. Very unusual here was the wharf's own dual-gauge internal railway system, standard gauge for normal traffic transhipped to and from the Cattewater Branch goods trains, and a broad gauge – of as far as I know – approximately seven feet mainly for the internal rail-mounted crane. This was completely independent of the GWR Broad Gauge, and had no connection with this in any way either physically or historically. The wharf's own standard-gauge shunting engine, waits patiently for its next duty with an impressive dual gauge point set in to the concrete. The view is looking west towards the limit of the line. *3 September 1991*

BELOW: It is quite refreshing to find, for a change, a location on the Cattewater Branch where the vista has barely changed, and is not overgrown or hidden by palisade fencing. With great thanks to the very friendly staff here, I was granted free access, and a conducted tour, of the scene today and the changes are indeed few. The dual-gauge point work is still there set in the concrete but unlikely ever to see another train. In both pictures the warehouses and the surrounding buildings other than a change of colour during repainting remain the same. At least the beginning and the end of the Cattewater Branch both remain, and with a familiar look at each location. In between those couple of miles of once very busy and under-photographed track and its quays and industry have largely been swept away. *4 September 2013*

VICTORIA WHARVES

ABOVE: The view looking from the end of the line back towards Cattewater Junction with the wharf's own diesel shunter patiently awaiting any further call to work. A fine opportunity to study the intricate dual-gauge point work embedded in the concrete. One cannot help but wonder if the road fork lifting truck has already taken over nearly all the work. The heavy duty crane looks impressive. To the left are the buildings housing the canteen and office block and Breakwater Hill provides the back drop. *3 September 1991*

BELOW: The main changes to the scene are the erection of further large warehouse storage units in the background mostly blocking the view of Breakwater Hill. The oil storage tanks to the right of these, situated by the former Western Fuels Siding, remain constant. The heavy-duty crane has been replaced by a more modern lightweight construction affair. The canteen and office block to the left is still there, but without the hanging baskets, and that wonderful dual-gauge point work is still set in the concrete as a reminder of the now long gone railway era from this still busy Wharf. *4 September 2013*

VICTORIA WHARVES - 'THE PLANET'

TOP: 'Yes it does work!' I must admit the outward appearance of this little engine does not fill one with confidence. The years of salt air, clay and other industrial dust had taken their toll. A few running repairs and it was up and running again.

'Planet' was the brand name applied to the small industrial diesel and petrol locomotives manufactured by M/S FC Hibberd and Co of Park Royal London. This particular Diesel Mechanical machine, works number 3281, was delivered to Victoria Wharf in 1948 making it one of the earliest diesels in the City, predating the first British Railways one in the area, Class 04 shunter number 11225, which arrived at Friary Shed on 7 September 1957, as the first of the replacements for the 'B4' shunting tank locomotives, by some nine years. The locomotive spent all its working life here at Victoria Wharf making it one of, if not the, longest-serving engines in the Plymouth area. Look behind the engine and another interesting feature can be seen, the head shunt which terminated in a dead-end tunnel under Teats Hill Road just by its junction with Commercial Road. This fulfilled the dual role of being the terminus of the Cattewater Branch and the shed for the 'Planet'. Few lines terminated in a tunnel which doubled as an engine shed, unique. *3 September 1991*

MIDDLE: With the loss of the short-lived China Clay traffic, rail activity sadly finished at Victoria Wharf which, of course, meant the 'Planet' diesel was redundant. I was able to purchase the locomotive on behalf of the Plym Valley Railway, and remember going round there with my late mother one fine Friday afternoon in October 1993 and presenting the cheque for £250. For the last time the Planet has left its shed and is being loaded on to a lorry for the journey over to Marsh Mills. Bill Ross and a much younger David Elbrow, two stalwarts of the PVR, are at rail level to cast a watchful eye on proceedings. The engine remains in store at the Plym Valley Railway in the queue for restoration, but not forgotten and one day our volunteers will return it to its former glory. *22 November 1993*

BOTTOM: Not much has really changed in the intervening years, the dead end tunnel head shunt marking the end of the line is still there, and the 'Planet' could almost emerge from it. Who knows one day it may even do so! *4 September 2013*

CATTEWATER JUNCTION, PLYMSTOCK BRANCH

We have already discussed and had a look at the view from the northern end of the Laira Road bridge of Cattewater Junction in relation to the Cattewater Branch. Now we turn our attention to the Plymstock Branch built from Cattewater Junction over the River Plym to Pomphlett, although the station was always known as Plymstock. This short stretch of railway was built by the re-awakened Plymouth & Dartmoor Railway acting as a spearhead for the London & South Western Railway. Although it is thought the Viaduct was completed in 1887, the line to Plymstock did not open until 5 September 1892.

TOP: The way things were when I first knew the area, a three-car DMU makes its way up the gradient from Cattewater Junction to cross the River Plym on its way to Plymstock. To the left the gate marking where the former Plymouth & Dartmoor Railway/ Lee Moor Tramway route crossed the Cattewater line is quite prominent.

MIDDLE: Things are starting to look a little less neat and tidy as a fairly rare visitor to Plymstock 'Class 37' Diesel 37 196 heads for Plymstock with the weed-killing train. Main line diesels were not a common sight here. This was one of the final trains to be seen at this location as total closure was not far away. *26 April 1987*

BOTTOM: The bridge span, the pylon to the left and the background houses provide a common link for the updated picture. Note the new footbridge allowing access to the present cycle path on the curve to Cattewater Junction. This looks a bit untidy but is liable to change in the near future as work gets under way to extend the cycle and foot path over the River Plym by way of the railway viaduct. *6 November 2011*

LAIRA VIADUCT FROM THE TRAIN

ABOVE: Looking across the viaduct from the carriage window towards Plymstock, I had taken the rare opportunity to join this train at Plymstock, not often one had had the opportunity since 1951 to become a genuine passenger there! The feature which stands out is the gas main on the left which runs the length of the viaduct, the latter looking a bit rusty at the time. There are some interesting buildings at Pomphlett in the background. *10 October 1970*

BELOW: Utilising the new cycle and footpath, almost a perfect update. The viaduct looks really the worse for wear after years of neglect, and the substantial barricade currently blocks any access to the structure. The gas main appears to be still there. This is a scene which should change for the better in the near future as work gets under way to convert the viaduct in to cycle and footpath extension over the River Plym towards Plymstock. *6 November 2011*

LAIRA RAILWAY VIADUCT FROM LAIRA ROAD BRIDGE

The new Laira road bridge was formally opened on 1 June 1962, its construction somewhat over-shadowed by its much larger neighbour at Saltash. Built along side the structure it replaced, the former 'Iron Bridge', it was also a very convenient point for photographing trains on the very close by railway viaduct.

RIGHT: Looking towards Plymstock, the Branch Line Society Plymouth Area Rail Tour three-car DMU crosses the Plym. The most notable land mark behind the train is the former Plymstock Cement Works to the left. *10 October 1970*

MIDDLE: Nothing changed much in the later years of the operational railway here. The Cement Works still dominate the background as 37 196 with its 'Tre Pol and Pen' (a true Cornish name indeed) nameplate clearly visible, heads away over the River. This really was a superb angle for railway photography. It is just a pity there were so few trains at a decent time to make good use of the facility. The viaduct looks in good shape but it would not be carrying trains for much longer. *26 April 1987*

BELOW: The Cement Works no longer dominates the back ground, I suspect before long some new housing will probably do so. The pylon is still there and the view looks very similar. The railway viaduct really shows the effects of years of salt and damp river air, wind and rain and general neglect, and it is very sad to see it has gone so rusty. However, as previously mentioned restoration work is now under way to restore the viaduct as part of the cycle and foot path extension, so hopefully in the near future this will be a scene transformed for the better. *6 November 2011*

LAIRA RAILWAY VIADUCT FROM LAIRA ROAD BRIDGE

The views are taken from what was the Plymstock end of the old Laira Road Bridge replaced in 1961 by the present structure. The abutment remains as a reminder of the former structure, and it was a good place for railway photography.

LEFT: Looking back towards Cattewater Junction, the branch Line Society Plymouth Area Rail Tour crosses the Plym on the approach to Plymstock. I remember thinking at the time when a DMU was a rare sight here what could have been had the passenger service survived, and how useful would that have been – and still be - with all the road works, congestion, traffic lights, bus lanes, etc.. This could have been a daily scene as I think the unit looks quite at home on the Railway Viaduct. *10 October 1970*

LEFT: A very rare visitor to the line and as far as I know, the only 'Hastings Diesel Electric Unit' ever seen here, the five-car Hertfordshire Rail Tours 'Gunnislake Goliath' Special formed of unit No. 1032 was also the last train to convey passengers over the Viaduct. The train was barred from entering Plymstock Station, and not much of it made it beyond the Viaduct. To ensure none of the passengers got off here, an unusual aspect was that the train conveyed a couple of British Transport Police Officers who ensured there was no illegal alighting or trespassing. In the declining light of the shortest day of the year, the train makes a very cautious approach to the Plymstock side of the river. *21 December 1985*

LEFT: Standing on the old road bridge abutment in the autumn sunshine, not much has really changed except for the condition of the railway viaduct. It does not look as if any restoration work has commenced on the structure, which rather sadly continues to rust quietly away. The Cattewater Junction pylon in the background is a common feature in all three images. *22 September 2011*

OLD LAIRA BRIDGE, THE RIDE AND CHELSON MEADOW

RIGHT: I am going to stick my neck out and state that is the only steam locomotive to have passed *under* the Plymstock Branch. This unique view was taken when 'Lee Moor No 2', and the restored former Tramway wagon, were in transit from the former Locomotive Shed at Torycombe for display at the 'Mayflower 70' Traction Engine Rally held that weekend at Chelson Meadow. In the foreground note the curve of the approach to the former Laira Road Bridge, and the bridge behind taking the railway over The Ride and Plymstock Cement Works is at the top of the hill. *17 July 1970*

RIGHT: The view is easily recognisable today with the abutment and approach to the former road bridge the common link between the two images. The railway over-bridge and the embankment which led to the former Plymstock Station have been demolished, and so has the former Cement Works. The pylon on the left is also another common feature. There is substantial tree growth and new buildings have sprung up here and there, but there is little to remind one that there was once a railway here. *22 September 2013*

RIGHT: 'Lee Moor No 2' was built to the unique Dartmoor four-foot six-inch gauge and was the second of two identical 0-4-0 Saddle Tanks delivered from Peckett & Sons, Bristol in 1899. The locomotives worked between the summit of the Cann Wood Incline near Plympton and the bottom of the second Torycombe Incline near Lee Moor until this section of the Tramway was closed from November 1945 when replaced by a pipe line. The engines remained in their shed at Torycombe and in 1964 when the Lee Moor Tramway Preservation Society was formed to preserve them. Lee Moor No 2 was the first to be cosmetically restored and was subsequently donated by the Clay Company to the Society which by now had amalgamated with the Plymouth Railway Circle who still own the little engine. Prior to going on display in an outhouse at Saltram for 31 years, the locomotive was displayed at the Traction Engine Rally at Chelson Meadow, and we were requested to provide 24-hour cover to look after it. Being the only one on the Committee who worked night shifts, I was volunteered for the dark hours and took this time exposure at about 0300 on the Sunday morning. I have not been back to the field to do an update! Sadly the engine was lost to Plymouth when relocated to the South Devon Railway at Buckfastleigh in Autumn 2001. *19 July 1970*

APPROACHING PLYMSTOCK

BELOW: A somewhat different view of the bridge over The Ride and the embankment leading to Plymstock Station from the previous page, taken on the hill beneath the former cement works. Plenty to look at in this image, starting behind the train where the Laira Railway Viaduct is mostly hidden behind the trees, the road bridge is to the left. Further left on the opposite side of the River Plym are Laira Wharf and Corporation Wharf, with the Plymouth 'B' Power Station (demolished September 1990 to February 1991) just creeping in to the picture. The Branch Line Society three-car DMU 'Mayflower Rail Tour' has halted for a photographic stop. *10 October 1970*

BELOW: Surprisingly some of the embankment on which the train was standing survives and provides the best link between the two images. Just in front of where the 3 car DMU was standing, there has been a breach to allow construction of the car park to serve 'The Range' and other nearby newly constructed retail units which have replaced the rather ramshackle buildings in the 'Then' image. Laira Road Bridge can just be picked out through the ever growing trees, the bank on the other side of the River Plym has altered substantially with the Marina replacing Laira and Corporation Wharfs. The view just about recognisable but there is not much evidence of the railway that existed here not that long ago. *6 November 2011*

PLYMOUTH 'B' POWER STATION

BELOW: I have inserted a second slightly different angle from the hill on the approach to Plymstock Station. This gives a better view of the former 'B' Power Station with its two chimneys on the other side of the River Plym, as we are about to make a couple of deviations away from railway matters and this is a good lead in to the first of them. On the tracks, 31 424 heads the annual weed-killing train with 37 299 on the rear, and it must be said, the Class 31 locomotives were not a common sight here. When one makes a study of a picture like this, one can only wonder how most of it looks so permanent, yet the majority of it has been swept away. *1 May 1982*

RIGHT: Just down the road by no more than half a mile or so, and on the other side of the railway lay Breakwater Road, where I climbed a mound one Sunday morning to get a grand stand view of the demolition of the two 'B' Power Station Chimneys. I got up early, and arrived a good two and a half hours before the main event to claim the best position on the highest rock. About five minutes before the demolition began, a very good crowd had assembled to witness the spectacle: then a couple of latecomers arrived, pushing their way through to the top, and a very arrogant lady demanded that I move 'because her husband had a cine camera'. My reply was possibly not the kindest I have ever uttered! Still intact, the chimneys await the moment. *28 October 1990*

Something different. I know it is deviating from the subject, my excuse is the Power Station was rail connected and did get some supplies by rail, and one does not get the chance to witness this sort of spectacle very often.

The charge is set.
Starting to go.
Going!

The second one starts to wane.
Nearly gone.
All gone.

Regretably, one person was killed by flying rubble on the other side of the River Plym from where I was standing. I extend my deepest sympathy to any relatives who may see this feature.
28 October 1990

PLYMOUTH BREAK WATER

TOP: The Red Arrows make a fine sight flying over one of the most distinctive land marks to be seen in Plymouth Sound. Countless people have stood on Plymouth Hoe and gazed out towards the Breakwater. I wonder how many of them have realised they are looking at the site of one of the earliest railways in the Country, and more than likely the first use of the train ferry principal in the world. *30 June 2012*

MIDDLE: The oldest 'Then ' picture in the book, and I have had to go back much further than the era of my 'Then' pictures based from the late 1950s onwards. There was a clue in the location for the pictures of the 'B' Power Station demolition and that is Breakwater Road. Work commenced on the much needed Plymouth Breakwater in 1812, and a three-foot six-inch gauge tramway was laid in Breakwater Quarry to Oreston Pier. Loaded trucks were able to run at most states of the tide directly on to ten or twelve boats (specifically designed by the engineers of the project John Rennie and Joseph Whidbey), and discharge their cargo into the sea. As the structure rose above water, as it almost certainly had sometime by 1814, rails were laid on the Breakwater and the first train ferry, anywhere in the world, was in use. Wagons were loaded in the quarry, shipped out to the Breakwater and transferred to the railway on the structure, and this became very useful and helped speed up completion of this massive project. About four million tons of stone were used, and the Breakwater cost £1.5 million, just shy of £85 million in today's terms. The engraving is undated, although it could possibly be 1840s.

BOTTOM: I organised a Plymouth Railway Circle outing to the Breakwater in August 1982. This image is based on the engraving above with the rusty, and somewhat corroded, rails clearly visible, and is looking east towards Bovisand with the light house behind me,. One can see a great deal of similarity in the two images despite there being more than a century and a half between them. While writing this book I met a gentleman who had been on the Breakwater earlier in the summer of 2013, and who informed me that the rails are still there and clearly visible. *August 1982*

PLYMSTOCK SIDINGS

BELOW: The view looking back towards Cattewater Junction of the sidings on the approach to Plymstock Station which is behind the photographer. The Class 31 Diesel stands with the weed-killing train, to the right is the relatively recent connection built in 1963, with a substantial cutting made in to the hill side, to serve the new Associated Portland Cement Manufacturers Ltd. Plymstock Works. This was still sending out traffic by rail (to Chacewater in Cornwall mainly) at this time. The other rail-borne traffic here at the time was LPG Gas, the depot is to the left with a goodly supply of wagons available. This busy-looking modern railway freight scene only had another three years before both sources of traffic were lost. *April 1984*

BELOW: The same scene today as yet undeveloped but one can only wonder how long that situation will last. The remaining ballast stones on the ground a clue to the former railway use, the contour of the hill on the right is perhaps the best link between the two images. *6 November 2011*

PLYMSTOCK CEMENT WORKS: 'THE VANGUARD'

TOP: With the completion of the short spur from Plymstock Station to the Cement Works, a brand new industrial locomotive was ordered to work within the Plant, and transfer wagons to and from the national system at Plymstock. Built by M/S Thomas Hill (Rotherham) Ltd. at their Vanguard Works, Kilnhurst, Yorks (hence the reason why the engine is known as 'The Vanguard') and the locomotive arrived at Plymstock in 1963 where it was to spend all its working industrial railway life. Technical details are: Weight 29 tons, Engine is a Rolls-Royce 6-cylinder diesel with Power of 175 hp. Wheel arrangement is 0-4-0 chain drive. The engine is seen here very much in the industrial setting of Plymstock Cement Works. *October 1987*

MIDDLE: A further view taken at the same time showing in particular the 'Vanguard's' purpose-built little engine shed to the right, and to the left a reminder of the solid rock through which the short spur to the Plymstock Branch ran. Again, with the Cement Works behind, a very industrial scene of which no trace remains today, and the site is being developed for housing. *October 1987*

BOTTOM: The Cement Traffic ceased at Plymstock late in 1987 and 'The Vanguard' was thus declared redundant. However, there is a happy ending to the story as the engine was placed in the care of the Plym Valley Railway and arrived at Marsh Mills at 1700 on Friday 30 March 1990, precision timing courtesy of the current Chairman of the Plym Valley Railway Association, Mr John Netherton. The engine was soon repainted in the familiar blue livery that we all, on the PVR, got very used to, and 'The Vanguard' has been a wonderful asset in the various stages of construction of the line to Plym Bridge. So this year sees the 50th Anniversary of this Industrial Locomotive which has given good service to two different railways in the City. With 'The Planet' from Victoria Wharf, yet again proof of the value of the PVR in preserving our local railway heritage. As I write these words, 'The Vanguard' is being repainted to provide brake van rides and enhance of the use of the line to Plym Bridge. *21 May 2008*

PLYMSTOCK STATION FROM ABOVE

The third of the aerial photographs obtained through the Plymouth Railway Circle, a birds-eye view of Plymstock Station in 1957. The view is looking south, the line from the Laira Viaduct enters from the bottom right. The rather traffic-free A379 runs almost alongside, with Pomphlett Creek and Breakwater Road adjacent, where the pictures of the Power Station Chimney demolition were taken from. The junction between the lines to Turnchapel and Yealmpton is clearly visible with coal wagons standing in a siding opposite the Turnchapel platform. A close up view of this part of the station will feature when we examine the Turnchapel Branch. The route to Turnchapel curves away crossing Pomphlett Road on Stamp's Bridge, this area, as we shall subsequently see, is now obliterated by Morrison's supermarket and McDonald's, the line heading towards Oreston in a cutting just by the sharp turn on Oreston Road. The line to Billacombe and Yealmpton - again we shall this section close up in subsequent pages - runs off to the bottom left of the picture. The Cement Works and the connecting line to it were yet to be built. The area certainly looks more rural then, for much has changed in the years since this fascinating image was taken. *27 June 1957*

PLYMSTOCK STATION – THE GREAT WESTERN SIDE

BELOW: It is by sheer coincidence that my picture, taken nine years after the one on the previous page, is a good partial update for the aerial view. The angle is again looking south and the former Turnchapel Branch, including its platform, has been demolished and swept away with hardly a trace. The first and much smaller Plymstock Roundabout has taken shape, traffic queuing not a problem then. The train, the Plymouth Railway Circle Plymouth Area Brake Van Rail Tour with D2178, is waiting where the Yealmpton Branch platform stood not so long before that, and, to the rear of the train, note the curve for the 1963 built connection through the hill to the Cement Works. The cliff edge of the quarry stands out, forming a natural basin, almost waiting for Morrison's to come along and fill it. *18 June 1966*

BELOW: Much has changed as we look south at Plymstock Station again. The viewpoint is the same, the common feature between the two images is the cliff edge, particularly visible to the left of the picture. There is no trace whatsoever of the station or any railway features, Plymstock roundabout, Morrison's supermarket and the McDonald's of today are mostly hidden by tree growth - I can assure you they are still there. Whether development will change this view in the near or long term future I am not able to say. One thing for certain it is totally different from the aerial view of 1957. *6 November 2011*

PLYMSTOCK STATION – THE GREAT WESTERN SIDE

BELOW: Plymstock Station was controlled by the Southern Railway who regarded the line to Turnchapel as 'The Main Line' and the GWR route to Yealmpton as 'The Branch.' The original signal box was burnt by incendiary bombs in the air raids of 1941, the structure seen below situated on the GWR Yealmpton platform being a 'temporary' replacement that lasted until closure on 1 May 1963. Note, behind it, the top of the signal on the Turnchapel Platform. Above the signal box legend 'Plymstock' the eagle-eyed will spot the name plate of the former North Road East signal box. The name plates from the six signal boxes taken over by the Plymouth Panel in November 1960 were stored here for a while, and brought out of storage one evening for the benefit of the photographers. *Summer 1961*

BELOW: A cracking view taken by an unknown photographer, which I only acquired, with copyright, whilst compiling this book, showing both platforms at Plymstock. To the left the DMU standing in the Yealmpton platform (and as far as I know the only one to traverse the length of both lines) is the 'Devon Rambler', a special run from Exeter by the Railway Enthusiasts Club of Farnborough who were active in this field for many years. Possibly the biggest crowd seen in many a year stands on the platform blocking the view of the signal box. To the right is the Turnchapel line platform with the inevitable coal wagon in the siding. Look beyond them and one can spot the starting signal with the Turnchapel lower arm distant as the line curves away towards Stamp's Bridge. A further view of this from a slightly different angle will feature when we examine the Turnchapel Branch. *11 April 1959*

PLYMSTOCK STATION – THE GREAT WESTERN SIDE

BELOW: Taken from almost the same angle as the 'Devon Rambler,' only seven years later, and the view is of another rail tour standing in the Yealmpton Branch platform, or, in this case, what had been the Yealmpton Branch platform. Much has changed with the demolition of both the Turnchapel side and the GWR platform. At least it still counts as a Yealmpton Branch picture. The spur to the Cement Works, opened on 25 September 1963, is clearly visible running off to the left of the picture behind the running lines where D2178 stands with the Plymouth Railway Circle Brake Van Tour *18 June 1966*

BELOW: To complete the set, the present-day image of what was Plymstock station, looking towards the former Yealmpton Branch platform. This is only a few yards out from the original views we have just been studying, but enough to convey the impression that nothing at all remains of the once busy Plymstock Station. *6 November 2011*

THE YEALMPTON BRANCH EAST OF PLYMSTOCK STATION

The line from Plymstock to Yealmpton was built by the Great Western. The general idea was that the LSW would build the extension to Modbury - but this never happened. Opened on 17 January 1898, the service was from Millbay and North Road. The line was an early casualty of road competition (mostly from GWR-operated buses!) and closed on 7 July 1930. To accommodate Plymouth people evacuated out in to the country, the line re-opened to passengers on 3 November 1941 and the service was from Friary. This ceased 7 October 1947 and the line closed completely with the withdrawal of goods facilities on 29 February 1960, a rare Leap Year Day closure. Only a short stub remained east of Plymstock and this saw little use, until the weed-killer and the photographers called one day.

LEFT: The track looks a bit rusty looking over the little iron bridge (which is still there somewhere amongst the growth) as 37 196 appears as if ready to depart for Yealmpton. A main line diesel here was a very rare visitor. An indication, perhaps, of what might have been. *26 April 1987*

LEFT: The train crew were only too happy to agree that the remains of the Yealmpton Branch needed some weed-killing treatment, so the train was taken, with some caution, to the absolute limit of the line. This is the nearest any main-line diesel got to Yealmpton. It cost me a few pints in the Railway Club that night, but that was well worth it for being able to run a main-line engine on the Yealmpton Branch. Priceless! Note how empty Billacombe Road and the roundabout seem to be. *26 April 1987*

LEFT: Such is the thickness and volume of growth, I was unable to find any path, or opening, to climb up and obtain a present-day shot from the same place. Even though the little iron bridge crossing the minor lane is still there - that too is shrouded in trees and vegetation. *4 September 2013*

BILLACOMBE STATION

Billacombe was the first station out from Plymstock on the Yealmpton Branch, situated by Moor Quarry and just by the junction of Colesdown Hill and the A379 where the latter changes from being Billacombe Road to Elburton Road.

LEFT: The view looking towards Yealmpton after closure. The Quarry Company seem to have waisted no time in improving access to their premises by laying a boarded crossing over the now derelict railway line. Previous access was cramped by the road under bridge seen on the left of the picture. *Summer 1961*

LEFT: The Quarry took over ownership of the station site and, towards the end of 1988, gave notice that they wished to demolish the remains of the former station so they could widen their private road, that had now been built along part of the track bed and through the former platform. The opportunity was given to the Plym Valley Railway to acquire the station building and work on dismantling the structure commenced on 2 April 1989. The task took two years. Each stone was individually numbered and transported as seen here in our trusty wagon to Marsh Mills. The Billacombe Station building will be rebuilt numbered stone by numbered stone on the completion of the new extension to the Marsh Mills platform, on which work is now underway. Yet another fine example of how the Plym Valley Railway is preserving the heritage of the city's railways. *April 1989*

LEFT: No trace remains of Billacombe station today and one could be forgiven for not realising the Yealmpton Branch once ran through here. Very careful study of the bottom two pictures reveals a minute portion of the wall on the hill on Elburton Road. Look to the extreme right of the station building and then compare below. That is the only clue to link the pictures *20 November 2011*

BILLACOMBE STATION FROM COLEDOWN HILL

BELOW: Although the track had long been lifted, when I first went over to Billacombe to record the first stages of the dismantling of the station building, I paid a visit to the bridge which took Colesdown Hill over the former Yealmpton Branch and obtained this rather attractive image showing the setting of Billacombe Station. The view is looking towards Yealmpton. The main A379 Elburton Road – still a proper dual carriage way then – is to the right, the little station is set quietly below, probably out of sight and out of mind. Trees hide the quarry which would be to the left of the picture. *April 1979*

BELOW: A repeat visit to the same location some 22 years later reveals the now familiar story of growth taking over the view. One can just about make out where the station used to be, some more buildings have appeared in the foreground on the former railway line, and the A379 Elburton Road can be picked out to the right. This, now, east-bound, is a single carriageway, prompting the question; 'what is the point of turning a road in to a much-needed dual carriageway, just to narrow it a few years later?' *20 November 2011*

ELBURTON CROSS

ABOVE: Not the best picture one will ever see of Elburton Cross Station, but one of the very few of it in colour. Taken after closure when the line was quietly rusting away: the view is looking towards Yealmpton. The Elburton Hotel is just out of camera range to the right. This station, as can be seen, was situated in a shallow cutting, and was very convenient for the village, and one can only wonder what use would have been made of it today. When I was a young clerk, newly started on the railway back in 1964, one of my elder colleagues in the Parcels Office, the late Bill Soper, told me of when he worked at both Billacombe and Elburton Cross stations in the 1930s. Apparently, even after the passenger service had ceased, the perishable traffic continued to be buoyant and, especially in the fruit and flower seasons, a clerk was still needed to waybill and process the accounts for the outgoing consignments, that were from local growers bound for the markets in London and big cities like Birmingham, Manchester and Liverpool. *Summer 1961*

ABOVE: The cutting has been filled in and today the station is very hard to identify unless one knows where to look, Elburton has no trace of its railway any more. Going from memory and working out where the line once ran, this view in the declining light of an autumn day is about as accurate as I can make it. The eagle-eyed will spot the telegraph poles that link the two images, left of centre. *20 November 2011*

YEALMPTON STATION

Although this is beyond the city boundary, I only really have one other decent colour picture of the line and that is at the terminus, so for the sake of continuity and to complete the job, a look at the former Yealmpton Station.

LEFT: A goat at Yealmpton. The last in a little sequence when Ivor Hocking, Keith Holt and myself did a visit to the line one fine summer's evening. This is the view looking towards the end of the line at the distant - and out of view - buffer stops. Yealmpton station was not designed as a terminus, it was built as a through station to accommodate the extension to Modbury - which was never built; the rails continued about a quarter of a mile to the over-bridge seen in the distance. This explains why the station was larger than would have been expected for a rural branch line terminus. To the right note the substantial, typical, GWR Goods Shed, and to the left, an imposing water tower. Sadly the weeds had by now taken over, but it was worth taking a rare view in colour to record a station which somehow never really lived up to expectations. *Summer 1961*

LEFT: The sad scene from almost the same spot as demolition of the station is well under way. The goods shed had already gone, the station building and canopy await the bulldozer, the lamp-man's hut, also visible in the top picture, looks a bit forlorn. Destruction of a railway is not the sort of scene I enjoyed witnessing, regrettably all too often similar scenes were repeated all over the West Country. *November 1971*

LEFT: Inevitably the station has now become a housing estate with no clue to the former use of the site, other than a commemorative plaque. I have included this rather ancient 'Now' picture as the background trees give some sort of continuity to the pictures. *August 1982*

PLYMSTOCK STATION – THE SOUTHERN PLATFORM

Plymstock Station was unique in that it was served by two railway companies, each physically isolated from its own system. Let me explain. By means of Running Powers, a legal rite granted by Parliament, any Southern (formerly LSWR) train to have reached Friary, and thus Plymstock, would have run over pure GWR metals from Devonport Junction to Friary Junction. Any GWR train, which would have run direct from Mount Gould Junction to Cattewater Junction over the Plymouth No 2 Curve closed and lifted in 1958, would have run over pure Southern metals from Cattewater Junction over the Laira Viaduct to reach Plymstock Station. It was all very complicated but it meant if I was writing this in 1913, passengers from Plymstock would have had a choice of about 60 trains a day over two routes into Plymouth with terminals almost adjacent to either end of the present City Centre. I wonder how useful that would be today.

ABOVE: Plymstock Station was controlled by the Southern who regarded their line to Turnchapel as 'The Main Line' and the GWR route to Yealmpton as 'The Branch'. The extension to Turnchapel opened 1 January 1897, passenger services ceased 10 September 1951 after a previous temporary closure due to a fuel crisis. Complete closure of the Turnchapel extension was in October 1961. So to the 'Main Line' as the Southern referred to it, 'M7' 30034 poses for the photographers on the occasion of the Plymouth Railway Circle Brake Van Special to mark the closure of the line to Turnchapel. The PRC target disc stands out well on the chimney of 30034. The GWR Yealmpton platform is behind the train with the signals for coming off the Yealmpton Branch prominent. Look to the right of the 'M7' and the roof of the previously mentioned signal box can just be glimpsed. *30 September 1961*

LEFT: The area has changed so much I could only try and work out where I stood to watch 30034. Standing in the middle of the Plymstock roundabout (and getting some strange looks from motorists) is just about bang on, but the elevation is lower due to the complete extermination of the former railway land here for road widening and improvements. *22 September 2013*

PLYMSTOCK STATION – THE SOUTHERN PLATFORM

ABOVE: Recalling the image of the 'Devon Rambler' DMU rail tour, discussed when we examined the GWR side at Plymstock, a view on the Turnchapel side taken as if one was standing in front of the two wagons parked up in the little siding to the right. This is a 'going away' shot of the PRC Brake Van Special with 30034, looking over the Billacombe Road bridge towards Oreston. A small clutch of photographers stand taking in the view seen on the previous page, not an orange or yellow jacket in sight. They did all move when the train went forward. *30 September 1961*

BELOW: It has changed so much here, with demolition of the embankment to make way for an enlarged Billacombe Road roundabout. The elevation has become lower, making it impossible to stand in the same place and do an exact update. This is still the view looking over Billacombe Road towards Oreston, it bears no resemblance to the original image. *22 September 2013*

ORESTON

LEFT: The station nameplate, long after the last passenger had passed by, introduces our next location.

BELOW: A picture kindly supplied by Tony Kingdom showing Oreston Station looking towards Plymstock just after the line had closed for good. It was a simple and attractive little station, no more than a glorified 'halt' but in its day it was useful for the nearby village. Note the former siding to the left behind the platform where coal traffic was handled until quite late in to the line's career. *October 1961*

RIGHT: An almost identical view taken four years later almost to the day. The track had been lifted a couple of yers earlier, but still standing in the autumn sunshine on the platform are the station nameboard and the typical Southern Railway concrete lamp posts, products of the former Exmouth Junction (Exeter) Concrete Works, and once so familiar all over the Southern system in the West Country. *October 1965*

RIGHT: The houses to the left and behind the former station confirm that this is the correct location for the updated image. There is hardly a trace to be seen of this once pretty little wayside stopping place and the track bed has become a footpath. *20 November 2011*

ORESTON – THE PLYMSTOCK DISTANT

RIGHT: Looking rather forlorn and surprisingly still in position on the Turnchapel side of Oreston Station, two years after the track had been lifted, and despite the fact the embankment on the approach to Plymstock Station had been razed to the ground for the road improvements, the distant signal for Plymstock is still in position. It will no longer warn any 'Up' trains of the need for caution and to be prepared to stop at the next signal ahead, which, in this case, would have been the 'home' signal for the Turnchapel platform at Plymstock. The signal is actually of the Western Region type so it would have been a very late-comer to the line, no doubt replacing a much older ex-LSWR one. This was a 'fixed' distant, i.e. one set permanently at caution and this was common practice on single lines. For a while it was a remarkable survivor. *October 1965*

RIGHT: Standing on the same Plymstock Road bridge today, vegetation dominates the scene, with even the view of the curve into the former Oreston station very restricted. The track bed at this point has become a footpath as far as the former Radford Crossing. *20 November 2011*

RIGHT: Shifting the present-day angle a little to the left to the top of the approach road to the former Oreston Station, the house just by the fixed distant signal in the 'Then' picture acts as a feature to link the two scenes. Notice, on the right of the station approach, the kerb is still laid with former rail as another clue to the former identity of the site. The actual track bed is to the right, hidden by all the foliage. *20 November 2011*

BAYLY'S WHARF, ORESTON

Not to be confused with the afore-mentioned Bayly's Wharf that was the terminus of the former GWR Sutton Harbour Branch. It is not surprising that in the Sutton Harbour/ Cattewater/Hooe Lake area with the many different wharfs and quays one would come across the duplication of names. What helps is that in the case of Bayly's Wharf, they were on different lines and served by different Railway companies

LEFT: So to the Southern-served Bayly's Wharf. Just before the Turnchapel line crossed Hooe Lake as we shall see shortly, the line split in to two with this very short 'branch from a branch' to serve the Plymouth & Oreston Timber Company at Bayly's Wharf, situated on the eastern shore of Hooe Lake. Pictures of the railway operating on this Bayly's Wharf are very hard to come by, and these two, taken by my great friend and mentor, Ivor Hocking, are the only two known colour pictures of this little-known railway byway. Just before closure, one of the Friary Shed allocated quartet of Class 03 Diesels - take your pick from D2175, D2176, D2177 or D2178 - pulls away from the wharf back towards the junction with the Turnchapel Branch and so onward to Plymstock. Notice the huge pile of rail chairs to the left, brought in to be placed on sleepers in the timber yard here, the finished product then going out by train to be used in relaying work all over the local railway system. When the line closed, the last train from Bayly's Wharf was a special for the BR Engineering Department, when Class 04 Shunter No 11228 brought the sleeper-chairing machine out for continued use on 26 October 1961. *August 1961*

ABOVE: Not much sign today of the curve leading out from Bayly's Wharf. With all the development here, this is as about as near as I could get to the original view. *4 September 2013*

BAYLY'S WHARF, ORESTON

BELOW: Of all the pictures we have seen of trains on the various industrial lines and wharfs around the River Plym, this one, to me, is the most evocative, as it really captures the flavour and essence of the quayside railway. Much wood is in evidence as the Class 03 Diesel waits for departure with an impressive load of timber. In the background on the far bank of the River Plym stands the industrial area of Cattedown, with the former Plymouth 'B' Power Station, then a prominent landmark, standing behind the former Corporation Wharf and Pethick's Quay. The Passage House Inn is in the picture as well - look to the extreme left behind the large pile of wood stacked by the chute. All over the country little quayside lines like this served all manner of local industries in their various forms. Now they are all gone - as has much of the industry they served. *August 1961*

RIGHT: Look to the right of the above image and in particular to the right of the elevated cabin. Just behind and mostly hidden by the tree one can just pick out the edge of a building, this is what I used as my landmark for the present-day picture. Everything has changed beyond recognition, not only has that busy quayside timber yard and its railway been swept away, the background has also been totally transformed. The Power Station was demolished 1990-1992, and the whole of the opposite bank of the River Plym at Cattedown has been transformed. Great changes all round. *4 September 2013*

HOOE LAKE SWING BRIDGE

RIGHT: The Turnchapel Branch reached its terminus, after the junction with the Bayly's Wharf line, by crossing Hooe Lake on a rather impressive swing bridge. This view is from the Oreston side looking across the structure towards Turnchapel. It was the middle section which actually swung to allow shipping entry to and from Hooe Lake. This was released by the Turnchapel signalman with a special key. He had to walk to the middle span to operate the machinery, and was marooned there until he cranked it shut again. Not too pleasant on a wet day I would imagine. *October 1961*

LEFT: The Hooe Lake swing bridge was demolished October-November 1963, and thus the only update one can achieve is to stand on the west bank of Hooe Lake and photograph the piers that remain. At the time of taking this view, Bayly's Wharf to the right was still busy with timber, although none of it would ever travel by rail again, and the Plymouth 'B' Power Station dominates the background. *December 1981*

LEFT: The scene all around the piers of the former Hooe Lake swing bridge has changed dramatically. The former Bayly's Wharf was to the right, the house I mentioned being the link for the picture of the train on the quay is a good pointer on the extreme edge, to connect this and the above image. The background on the Cattewater side is, as we have already seen, now completely different - the Power Station was a significant local landmark. Look inland to the right of this, the houses of the St Judes and Lipson areas of the city on the distant hill are another link in this much-changed scene. *4 September 2013*

ENTERING TURNCHAPEL STATION

BELOW: 30034 enters Turnchapel Station with the Plymouth Railway Circle Brake Van special for the second time. Photographic run-pasts for participants on Rail Tours are nothing new. The train is coming off the Hooe Lake Swing Bridge, the view of which rather sadly is blocked by the concrete post to the right of the train (0 out of 10 for that one!) and is just about to pass the little signal box. Bayly's Wharf with all its timber is on the opposite bank to the left. *30 September 1961*

BELOW: As we shall see, the site of Turnchapel station is now being developed for new housing, so this scene will alter greatly in a very short period of time. I can only deal with the here-and-now when updating pictures. There has been a reduction in levels with the removal of the former railway at this point, but the piers of the former Hooe Lake swing bridge reveal this to be the same angle. Much has changed on both sides of the Lake, and will continue to do so on this side. On the opposite bank Bayly's Wharf was to the left. Hard now to imagine that this was where 30034 came into the Station. *4 September 2013*

TURNCHAPEL STATION

ABOVE: 30034 poses in the platform at Turnchapel with the Plymouth Railway Circle Brake Van Special - the view is looking towards Plymstock. The gentleman speaking with the train driver is the cameraman from Westward Television, who had only recently started broadcasting in Devon and Cornwall and they covered the Special with what is now some precious vintage film. There was a report and pictures of the train on Westward Diary two days later on the Monday. *30 September 1961*

BELOW: After the closure of the line and lifting of the track, Turnchapel Station was taken over by the adjacent British Gas Corporation, and incorporated into their oil storage depot. Just four years after seeing 30034 stood in this position at the simple little platform, similar in design to that at Oreston, oil pipes have arrived as a prelude to the new use of the site. The station was demolished shortly after I took this view. An updated present day image will accompany the picture on the next page. *October 1965*

TURNCHAPEL STATION

ABOVE: Taken a few yards further down the line, I could not resist including a further picture of 30034 at Turnchapel as it catches the atmosphere of 1960s-type rail tours on lines already closed to passengers, and those about to close for good. 30034 has been detached from its brake vans prior to running round the train for the return journey back to Friary. There is a very relaxed sort of feeling as people stand and observe the proceedings, and others take advantage of a convenient signal for a higher elevation. Back then no-one batted an eyelid about such goings on. Common sense prevailed and everyone went away safe and happy. *30 September 1961*

BELOW: Since the two 'Then' pictures were taken so close to each other and both look the same way, I offer this image as the update for both. With the station site now levelled and work underway with a new housing development, there is precious little to go on, and I could only really go back as far as I could and use my memory to try and work out the length of the 30034-hauled train and then add a few yards, so this is the best I could do. I probably needed to go back a few yards more but that was impossible due to a sudden change in levels behind me. My thanks to the helpful foreman and the builders of this Barratt Homes 'Reflections' development, who signed me in, issued me with a hard hat and were happy to escort me to wherever I wanted to go. This a scene that will change again in the very near future. *4 September 2013*

TURNCHAPEL STATION

RIGHT: A view of the simple little platform built on a gentle curve looking towards the end of the line. There is no mistaking the location, the weathered name board tells us we are at Turnchapel. The signal that we saw participants in the 30034 rail tour climbing on, for the different view, is on the end of the platform. It had been a decade since the passenger service had been withdrawn, the station does look a bit run down but at least it was still there. Not a lot of cover from the elements on offer! *August 1961*

RIGHT: Activity at Turnchapel with a rear-end view of the Plymouth Railway Circle Brake Van Tour. Steam from 30034 can be spotted at the front of the train. People travelling on this rail tour would be the last passengers at Turnchapel. One face I can pick out on the veranda of the nearest brake van to the camera is the gent to the left, the late Dick Toby, a stalwart member of the Plymouth Railway Circle who worked at M Thomas Motors. To the right in both images note the secure fence protecting the Gas Corporation oil storage depot which would soon engulf the station site. *30 September 1961*

RIGHT: Visiting the station site as the new housing development got under way, looking in this direction the obvious landmark is the large rock situated on the end of the platform and right next to the signal in the upper picture. It is a very useful link between the two 'Then' images and the view as seen in 2013. Let us hope this will survive the housing development and be a marker for future generations to pick out the site of the former Turnchapel station. *4 September 2013*

TURNCHAPEL ADMIRALTY WHARF

LEFT: I suspect few people in Turnchapel and certainly more in Plymouth are unaware that there is a short tunnel under Boringdon Road leading out on to the former railway that served Turnchapel Wharves. This was the main part of the 500-yard extension from Turnchapel Station, and was always freight only. *1961*

RIGHT: Turnchapel Wharf was built originally to serve M/S Bulteel, and was taken over by the Admiralty during the First World War, who retained custody right up until the departure of the Royal Marines from here in 2013. I was very surprised to find, some nine years after the line had closed, that most of the track on Admiralty Wharf was still intact, complete with a former small crane wagon still on the rails. The eagle-eyed can follow the track out onto the quay. The Cattedown area is on the opposite bank of the River Plym. Breakwater Hill can be spotted to the left to give some bearings to the location. *August 1970*

RIGHT: Admiralty Wharf as seen in its last days of use by the Senior Service, adapted by the Royal Marines with a good display of their landing craft and other equipment on show. Naval use of the quay finished with the departure of the Royal Marines to their new base in Devonport Dockyard opened by HRH Prince Harry on 2 August 2013. No doubt this is a scene that will change sometime soon. As to what will happen to Admiralty Wharf is, as far as far as I know yet to be decided, no doubt there will be some form of public access, and I hope that includes the former railway tunnel as I would like to get an exact update of that one. This was the terminus of the Turnchapel Branch and concludes our examination of, not only the Turnchapel Branch, but also the other lines that were served by Friary Station. *6 November 2011*

LAIRA DIESEL DEPOT

We move on to the former concrete foot-bridge seen to the right of the 'Then' photograph at the top of page 19, so I will commence this stage of our journey geographically, as opposed to Laira Shed chronologically, and have a look at the Diesel Depot. This was built on the site of Laira Freight Yard which closed in 1958. The depot came in to use towards the end of 1961 and was formally opened on 13 March 1962. With the ex-Great Western Lines west of Taunton amongst the first to be dieselised under the BR 1955 Modernisation Plan, this was very much a flagship of the new order.

TOP: Two shots from the Diesel Hydraulic era, enough to set many railway enthusiasts wallowing in nostalgia. After the end of steam in the 1960, many railway photographers put their cameras away or headed for pastures new in Europe. I am glad I kept mine going as pictures from this period are possibly the most sought after in railway history. Laira Diesel Depot in its early years is very much associated with Hydraulic Traction and whose story and downfall is beyond the scope of this book. D6323 with an unidentified Class 52 'Western', behind, as seen from the concrete footbridge standing by the fuelling point. The Diesel Depot is behind, on the right of the structure, the three road servicing shed, this was demolished in 1979 to make way for the HST Maintenance and Servicing shed, this further extended in the 1990s for the ill-fated 'Night Star' European services intended to run with the opening of the Channel Tunnel. Plymouth never did get its proposed Plymouth-Paris sleeper train and lost the one it did have to Glasgow and Edinburgh. The former steam shed was to the left background where the DMUs are berthed. *May 1971*

MIDDLE: A view a couple of years later taken a little more to the right with a good display of 'Westerns' on Shed. Notice how the former double-track line from Mount Gould Junction to Laira cuts through the sidings. When this was diverted to the former 'Speedway' in 1978, the sidings were joined up, now giving a very substantial storage area for HSTs running parallel to the Depot. *6 November 1973*

BOTTOM: With no footbridge, and fencing and growth prevailing, this is the best I can do today. *29 September 2013*

LAIRA STEAM SHED

The Steam Locomotive Depot at Laira opened in 1901 and was constructed to the GWR pattern of the time, being similar to Taunton (opened in 1896), and Croes Newydd, Wrexham (opened a year later in 1902). Like the latter, Laira was built within a triangle of lines, fitting into the parcel of land enclosed by the main line, the Sutton Harbour Branch and the Lipson No 1 Curve. Much of the land had been reclaimed from the River Plym over a period of years. The Shed closed to steam traction in October 1964 and demolition commenced on 14 December 1966. No trace of it remains today. Under the British Railways Shed Code Numbering system introduced in 1950, Laira became 83D in August 1950 as one of the sheds in the Newton Abbot Motive Power Division. By September 1963 when steam had all but been eliminated from the former GWR lines in Devon and Cornwall and the Motive Power Superintendant's Office at Newton Abbot closed, Laira was re-coded as 84A, recognising its importance as the main depot in the West of England. Today the HST sets allocated to the Diesel Depot for maintenance purposes have reverted to the former GWR 'LA' prefix. A few Laira memories are recorded on this on the following pages more or less in date order since I came to know the Shed.

ABOVE: Laira, the lair of Kings for this the greatest of all the GWR 4-6-0- classes had a long association with the Depot from their introduction in 1927 to their demise in 1962. 6027 'King Richard I,' a Laira-allocated engine at the time, is seen having come on Shed and probably waiting its turn for the coaling stage. *26 July 1959*

ABOVE: Maid of all work 2-6-0 4300 class 'Mogul' 6301 stabled opposite the coaling stage. They were often used at this period on one of the 'inter change' turns, working one of the two turns by Western Region men over the former Southern route via Okehampton introduced in the Second War, so that each had knowledge of the other's route in case of emergency. One cannot overstate how important that would be in this day and age when the Dawlish-Teignmouth sea wall becomes a victim of Mother Nature. *3 August 1959.*

LAIRA SHED –MORE MEMORIES OF STEAM (LAST KING AT LAIRA)

RIGHT: Another familiar long term resident of Laira Steam Shed 0-6-0 6400 Class auto fitted (i.e. able to push/pull its train) tank No 6421 ready to take water by the coaling stage. The class was introduced in 1932 and this engine spent most of its working life allocated to Laira, for use on the intensive suburban service to Saltash, with extensions to various stations to Liskeard, which were mostly dieselised in June 1960 with steam finishing completely at the close of 1962. These locomotives also worked in fits and starts with the auto trains which ran up the branch via Yelverton to Tavistock South. *September 1959*

RIGHT: As far as I know, and I stand to be corrected on this one, this was the last 'King' to be seen at Laira. On 27 January 1962 we had the rare event of Plymouth Argyle reaching the 4th-Round of the FA Cup and an attractive home tie against Tottenham Hotspur, who were then, like now, one of the top teams in the country. Seeing Argyle get beyond the first round is an achievement these days, but in 1962, the club were riding high in the second tier of English football and a number of special trains were laid on to bring 'Spurs' supporters down for the match, some of which were steam hauled and proved to be, as far as I know, the last time a 'King' worked a train in or out of Plymouth. It was a bitterly cold day, and having to make the choice between going to the match or seeing the steam, the latter was the chosen option. There is still frost lying where the sun could not penetrate, here we see 6018 'King Henry VI' being prepared in the afternoon on Laira Shed, behind the coaling stage, to work one of the specials back to London, with part of the rather ancient-looking vehicles of the Laira Break Down Train alongside. It was not a happy day seeing the last 'King' at Laira, nor was it too good for the Argyle fans, as the home team lost 5-1. *27 January 1962*

BOTTOM: Taken a little further to the right of the picture of 6018, the coaling stage was just to the left, the straight track of the entrance to 'The Speedway' to the right of 6018 and the through line of today confirm that we are in the same area. The present-day view is hardly inspiring. *26 October 2012*

LEFT: Another long-term resident of Laira Shed, and one we have already encountered on a rail tour on the Sutton Harbour branch, 1361 Class 0-6-0 Saddle Tank 1363 stands at the foot of the coaling stage, probably engaged on coaling stage duties pushing the loaded coal wagons up and bringing the empties down. For many years these gallant little engines were more associated with dock shunting - especially at Millbay. The changing scene as we move on in 1962 and the newly opened Diesel Depot can be seen behind 1363. This engine was allocated to Laira Shed from at least August 1950 until withdrawn in January 1963. The engine was sold into preservation firstly on the Quay at Totnes, then at Bodmin General Shed and now part of the Great Western Society Collection at Didcot Shed. An ideal candidate to visit the Plym Valley Railway one day. *24 June 1962*

LEFT: The same summer but steam is getting a bit thin on the ground. We are looking west towards the Round House with 'Manor Class' 4-6-0 7805 'Broome Manor,' the houses in Brandon Road are a landmark. I remember it was up there to the right somewhere in a little hall in the 1950s that my sister attended Delva Headon's Dancing Class. With no one to look after me, I got dragged along one day, and told to sit in the corner, only to find a grandstand view of Laira coaling stage and the main line on offer. After that I was more keen on going to dancing class than my sister! *June 1962*

LEFT: In the bleak midwinter of early 1963, one cold and frosty morning we see 'Hall' Class 4-6-0 no 6924 'Grantley Hall' outside the Round House, with the wheel hoist visible behind the locomotive tender. On closure of the Shed to steam this went to Cardiff Canton. There was something about that sound of hissing steam and piston crank. Laira School, on the skyline to the right, is a good landmark. *26 January 1963*

LAIRA SHED – THE COALING STAGE.

RIGHT: A veritable line-up of locomotives at the coaling stage on a spring evening, and probably one of the last occasions one would have seen such a gathering of steam here, as, by now, diesels had made serious inroads on to the scene. Lined up are: 7924 'Thornycroft Hall,' 4978 'Westwood Hall', 6921 'Borwick Hall', 'Mogul' 6346, and as we shall see later, 7022 'Hereford Castle.' The engines came on Shed and took coal, here also was the pit where ash from the smoke box and fire was dropped. Here then one example of how the labour market influenced the phasing out of steam. Many see the steam age through rose-tinted spectacles, but in reality it was unpleasant work. Employing men at £7 a week to work in pits such as this, with all the filth and dust, was becoming a recruitment problem, especially as the office and factory jobs available in the late-1950s and 1960s became more attractive, with the better pay, cleaner conditions and better hours. I remember one of my former colleagues telling me, on retirement many years ago, that working on the ash pits at Laira Shed at three o'clock in the morning on a wet and windy winter's night was no pleasure, and that many of the men were glad to see the back of steam. *3 April 1963*

RIGHT: A gem of a view from the coaling stage looking towards Laira Junction with a very clean 2-8-0 2800 Class no 3849 in the foreground. We are looking towards Laira Junction with an impressive display of signals. The signal box is to the extreme right and behind is the Embankment Road over-bridge that we shall be visiting shortly. The houses of the Laira estate are to the left. *August 1961*

RIGHT: The scene is not so attractive these days, all traces of the coaling stage and the ash pits have long since been swept away. This part of the Shed, at present, is used for stock storage. The houses to the left are a good link between this and the middle image as their outline is broadly similar. Like everywhere else, the trees have grown up here as well. *26 October 2012*

LAIRA - THE LONG SHED

The Long, or New, Shed was added in 1931 and was in full use by 14 February 1932. It was constructed at the same time as other improvements to the Shed, the main one being provision of 'The Speedway' to give greater flexibility of movements to and from the Depot. It was built between the Stores and the Round House and was straight with four lines. This was really the home of the main line 4-6-0s and was almost purpose-built.

When the first diesels arrived on Laira Shed in 1958, they were stabled and maintained here. A curtain running the length of the Shed was put up in the middle, with two lines being the temporary diesel depot until the new purpose-built diesel depot became available towards the end of 1961. This was a far from satisfactory situation, and did nothing to enhance the performance of the early 'Warships' and the D63XX class.

LEFT: A clean and shining 6863 'Dolhywel Grange' outside the Long Shed. These 4-6-0s were regular performers on the Cornish main-line to which they were ideally suited. It is a great pity none were preserved. *August 1961*

LEFT: We move on a couple of years towards the end of the steam era with 5975 'Winslow Hall' prominent outside the Long Shed amongst a gathering of various ex-GWR 4-6-0s. By now the steam engines were getting rundown, and standards, particularly with regard to appearance and condition, were allowed to slip - sadly, all too obvious in this view. *August 1963*

LEFT: Almost the same view today, the houses in the background to the right provide a link between this and the above image. There is no trace of the Round House or the Long Shed to be seen,as this part of the Depot now mainly used for stock storage. *26 October 2012*

LAIRA SHED – THE LAST BREATHS OF STEAM 1964

LEFT: By 1964 ex-GWR steam was a rare sight at Laira as the rundown of steam on the Western Region took a fierce hold. This was reflected in the condition of many of the locomotives which continued to deteriorate. Here we see a rather scruffy 4-6-0 'Modified Hall' 6988 'Swithland Hall' with the Long Shed behind. *2 April 1964*

LEFT: A glorious last fling. 7029 'Clun Castle' being prepared outside the Long Shed for the epic return run of the Ian Allan high-speed 'Castle'-hauled rail tour, 1Z48 1620 Plymouth-Paddington, run to mark the 60th Anniversary of 'City of Truro' achieving the first 100mph on rails descending Wellington Bank towards Taunton with an 'Up' Ocean Mail Express. This was the last (as far as I know) 'Castle'-hauled train to depart from Plymouth, and the run back to Bristol and London has gone down in the annals of railway history. Indeed it was a leading factor in the private purchase of 7029 for preservation. The way things were, a gleaming 7029 outside the Long Shed. *9 May 1964*

LEFT: A broadside view of the same engine on the same occasion. Engine men taking a pride in the job, with a few enthusiasts about. A gleaming 'Castle' was such a contrast to the rundown appearance of the remaining steam engines. When 7029 came off Shed to work that special, it was the end of an era. *9 May 1964*

LAIRA SHED – THE LAST BREATHS OF STEAM 1964

ABOVE: For the remainder of the summer of 1964, the only steam engines to be seen at Laira were the handful which worked over the former Southern route via Okehampton, until steam officially finished on this route on 7 September 1964. Outcasts from Friary could be one description that fits the bill. Bulleid Pacific 'Battle of Britain' Class 4-6-2 No 34081 '92 Squadron' takes on a further supply of coal. With the piles of ash around, and coal wagons on top of the coaling stage, one could be led to thinking this was a busy shed scene. Sadly the Southern interlopers, that one could count on the fingers of one hand, were all that was to be seen. *May 1964*

BELOW: Ivor Hocking, Keith Holt and I regularly met at Laira Shed at least once a week at lunch time to see and photograph any steam that may have been around. A typical lunchtime view of the period with British Railways Standard Class 4 75022 stood outside the empty Round House alongside 'Ivatt 'Tank 41317 which would work the 1709 Plymouth to Gunnislake, this being one of the Callington Branch engines that worked in for servicing. I was a bit annoyed to have got a fellow photographer in the picture: on the right is the late Keith Holt, who was the City Archivist at the time – but all these years on does it matter? Nice to pay tribute to someone whose work is included in this book. *July 1964*

ABOVE: What better way to bid farewell to steam at Laira than to go back to one of those many evening visits, this time in April 1963 to view the sun set on the age of steam. During spring and summer, late in the day, the sun came round far enough to glisten upon any engines parked up on the east end of the coaling stage. Basking in the last rays of the setting sun, we see 7022 'Hereford Castle', 'Mogul' 6346 and 6921 'Borwick Hall'. 7022 was the last 'Castle' allocated to Laira, and spent most of the summer of 1963 on one of the last 'Castle' turns, the weekday Saltash to Goodrington excursion. My parents I am glad to say were not opposed to my suggestion that we were regular day trippers to Torbay that summer, the direct service they thought was most convenient. Sun set on the age of steam at Laira, nice one Mr. Holt. *3 April 1963*

BELOW: After closure to steam in October 1964, the steam shed stood as a deserted and, at times, a seemingly melancholy empty shell until demolition began in December 1966. The new order was established as 'Western' Class Diesel D1004 Western Crusader', one of the seven originally experimentally painted in green livery, passes the deserted steam shed on the former 'Down' Lipson Loop light engine Laira Shed, to Plymouth Station to work an 'Up' London express. The track to the top of the coaling stage has already been lifted. Behind stands the Round House with the New, or Long, Shed alongside to the left. Where, not so long ago, there was hustle and bustle, and the sound and smell of steam, there were now just weeds, stony silence, and memories. An updated view of this scene cen be seen on the next page. *15 August 1965*

LAIRA JUNCTION

ABOVE: We now move on to the Embankment Road Bridge to study the changing scene of Laira Junction over the years. I will start on the south end of the bridge with particular reference to the junction for the Sutton Harbour Branch and the Shed. A rather sad occasion as 'Western' Class D1013 'Western Ranger' comes home to Laira Depot for the last time, shorn of its name and number plates after working (with D1023) the 'Western Tribute' rail tour the previous day, the very last 'Western' -hauled train, and in the case of Plymouth only 13 years since the last 'Castle' hauled one with 7029. The hydraulic age was indeed cut very short. A forlorn D1009 'Western Invader' has been parked in the carriage sidings for stock-warming duties. The Sutton Harbour Branch double track to Mount Gould Junction is the second set of points. Behind we have a fine view of the 1962 Diesel depot with an array of motive power on Shed. Come to the right and the former steam shed is seen in use as a dumping ground for withdrawn 'Westerns' and further stock storage. The coaling stage where we saw 7022 and D1004 on the previous page was just to the right of the little red-brick building seen by the red vehicles of the breakdown train. *27 February 1977*

ABOVE: The updated scene of today with a lot of tree growth, the diesel depot to the left has seen the servicing shed replaced by the 1982 HST Shed, and stock is still stabled on the former steam shed. *3 August 2013*

ABOVE: The more traditional view of an 'Up' train passing Laira Junction with D1001 'Western Pathfinder' heading 1A48 1055 Penzance to Paddington Cornish Riviera Express. Laira Junction Signal Box is to the left, for many years one of the resident signalmen here was the well-known Larry Crosier, a great personal friend and former Secretary of the Plymouth Railway Circle. To many this was simply known as 'Larry's Box'. The former 'Up' Sidings where the auto coaches for the Saltash and Tavistock services were stabled were to the right, the former steam shed was to the top left. The signals in the foreground controlled movements off the Lipson Loop, Sutton Harbour Branch, and off the Shed. *May 1971*

BELOW: Laira Junction Signal Box closed 10 November 1973 when control of the area passed to the Plymouth Station Power Box. Its site is marked by the rather austere relay room, otherwise changes are few. The 'Up' Cornish Riviera passes but now it is an High Speed Train, these having been introduced to the service in 1979, and I think they look very smart in their original blue and grey livery. *December 1982*

ABOVE: Enter the era of the privatised railway, in this case the time when Virgin Trains had been awarded the Cross Country franchise and the final days of daytime locomotive-hauled services. There have been a few changes in the 20-odd years since the previous picture was taken, the main one being that the site of the former 'Up' sidings on the right has been given over to a housing development, and a few bushes have appeared in between the tracks by the relay room. The uniquely 'Police' liveried Class 47 Diesel 47 829 heads away from the City with the 1150 to Liverpool, a Virgin HST waits to come off the former steam shed. *26 March 2002*

ABOVE: So to the present day where the main changes are - the erection of the Network Rail radio mast to the right, and a large tree blocking most of the view of the houses where the 'Up' sidings once existed. It looks like someone has done some successful weed killing by the relay room. In First Great Western livery - worth contrasting with blue and grey - 43086 front and 43131 rear have charge of 1A85 1100 Penzance-Paddington, the present-day 'Cornish Riviera'. *3 August 2013*

LAIRA JUNCTION – A LOW LEVEL VIEW.

ABOVE: An extremely rare visitor passing slowly along the 'Up' main line is PWM 652, one of the five members of Class 97/6. These 0-6-0 diesel shunting locomotives were purpose-built by Ruston & Hornsby of Lincoln for departmental (i.e. engineering) duties hence their numbering denoting engineering use. PWM 652 spent most of its life working in Fairwater Yard at Taunton, and was very rarely seen away from there. On this occasion it had been used for relaying work in Cornwall. Quite why the Civil Engineer went to the trouble of bringing the engine down rather than use the motive power which would have come with the necessary engineering/track train is unknown. This little engine was withdrawn in 1987 and scrapped in 1990. The shot is taken in declining evening autumn light from the former Lee Moor Tramway where it crossed the main line. The boarded-in wooden crossing had been removed in October 1960. A fine study of Laira Junction signal box as well. *October 1965*

ABOVE: :Not much of a view of the main line, Laira Junction or anything else for that matter these days. You just have to take my word that I am standing in the same place. *3 August 2013*

THE LEE MOOR TRAMWAY AT LAIRA

Time for a brief history lesson as, in later years, this was referred to as the Lee Moor Tramway, but it wasn't initially. The Plymouth & Dartmoor Railway opened its four-foot six-inch gauge horse-worked line from Sutton Harbour to King Tor (near Princetown) on 26 September 1823. From this line at a point by the Rising Sun Inn, now buried under the Marsh Mills Roundabout, a branch was opened to Cann Quarry on 20 November 1829. From this later line a further branch was built from a junction near Plym Bridge in 1854 to Lee Moor, and this was the Lee Moor Tramway. When the Plymouth & Dartmoor and the Cann Quarry Lines closed in 1900, this left only the Lee Moor Tramway which then became incorporated into the remaining sections of the former lines until its final closure in 1960. By the time I arrived on the scene this had been referred to as the Lee Moor Tramway for many years.

ABOVE: Turning around 180 degrees from the previous shot, there is still evidence of the Lee Moor Tramway with the rails on the extreme bottom right still visible. The view is looking from the main line towards the former Laira Inn where I had many a pint with Mr Crosier! I think I am correct in saying that locals knew this road as 'the Laira Dip'. The original Laira roundabout can just be spotted on top to the right of the pub. *October 1970*

RIGHT: With the roadworks of the early 1970s and filling-in of the ground, add on the years of growth and there is little to see at the present time. A couple of houses which can be picked out in the trees to the right actually form a link between the two images. *3 August 2013*

ABOVE: The Lee Moor Tramway had its own bridge under Embankment Road, and this looks a fairly modern structure. I have been unable to ascertain a date for construction of this, it certainly didn't come with the line in 1823! I am standing just behind the Laira Inn which is to the left, looking up towards the former Laira Roundabout. On the other side of the bridge the tramway ran alongside the inlet on a little wharf. This is a rather untidy view, possibly the demolished building a sign of things to come as this area was soon to be transformed by major roadworks. *October 1970*

BELOW: All traces of the Lee Moor Tramway, the 'Laira Dip' and, regrettably, the pub, have been swept away by the roadworks of the early 1970s. The slip road from Embankment Road towards the Laira Narrows and Mutley direction has overtaken the site of where the Lee Moor Tramway once passed under the road, and now an enlarged concrete bridge has replaced the original iron structure. *3 August 2013*

ABOVE: A somewhat different and unusual view from the Embankment Road Bridge looking down on the site of the Lee Moor Tramway main line crossing. The pictures of PWM 652 and the 'Laira Dip' were taken by the railings behind the mile-post. The most notable feature is of course the double arm bracket signal controlling the relief lines behind Laira Junction signal box. Silent sentinels – a term often applied to the traditional mechanical signals once such a familiar scene on our railways. Behind, work is under way in Old Laira Road on the alterations and construction of the new road system here. The signal was removed just four days after this shot was taken. *6 November 1973*

ABOVE: The scene is still recognisable although all traces of the Lee Moor Tramway have been removed and vegetation blocks most of the view of Laira Road Road. Perhaps the most notable differences in the two images are the colour of the house on the end of Laira Avenue, and the wall that replaced the railings by the railway line. The 244-mile post from Paddington (via Bristol and the Weston-Super-Mare Avoiding Line) has been renewed, the replacement now looking a little weathered. Our railways are still measured in miles and chains as opposed to the metric system that many are trying to introduce. Although the direct route from here to London is just over 20 miles less, the mileposts west of Taunton continue with the posting from Paddington on the original line. It was not until 1904 the route through Castle Cary was completed, meaning the observant on a train from Paddington to Plymouth will notice the train will run under five different measures from Paddington. Railways and their history can be complicated at times. *3 August 2013*

LAIRA CAUSEWAY

Possibly one of the most fondly remembered features of the area was the Causeway at Laira, and the little tidal inlet with Blagdon's Boat Yard and Wharf once served by the horse-drawn wagons of the Plymouth & Dartmoor Railway, later the Lee Moor Tramway.

ABOVE: The classic view from the south end of the Embankment Road Bridge looking east with 'Warship' Class D867 'Zenith' coming off Laira Shed. The engine is on the loop line, the 'Up' and 'Down' main lines are to the left of the engine. It is high tide at Laira with plenty of water in the little harbour to the left. The brand new Plympton Bypass can be spotted in the far back ground, a sign of the further road building to come in the city which would soon transform this tranquil scene. *September 1970*

BELOW: The changing scene at Laira with the former tidal inlet filled in, and the boat yard is no more. Bridgeworks and road construction for the dual carriageway through Crabtree are by now well advanced. Changes on the rails were afoot too, as just four days after this picture of D1000 'Western Enterprise,' the first of the Class, working light engine into Plymouth to take over the 'Down' Cornishman from 'Peak' D125 was taken, the signals were abolished as the area was put under the control of the Plymouth Station Panel, and colour light-signalling was introduced. *6 November 1973*

LAIRA CAUSEWAY

BELOW: For the best colours and clarity, there is nothing like strong winter sunlight. The problem is finding it! The morning mists have just cleared from the River Plym as a 'Down' HST approaches Laira Junction. The scene on the river Plym has changed little, perhaps the wreck of the Antelope, to the far right, has rotted away a bit more. On the railway, the signals have been replaced by colour lights. To the left, the new road layout, completed about seven years earlier, has settled down to the layout so familiar today, one would never know that the inlet and Blagdon's Boat Yard was ever there. *December 1982*

BELOW: The scene has a familiar look about it today, the main difference is of course the growth of vegetation. The wreck in the River Plym has shrunk a bit more. An interesting combination on the rails with a couple of preserved steam engines ex-GWR 5029 'Nunney Castle' (an ex Laira engine) piloting ex-LNER 'A4' 60019 'Bittern' double heading 1Z29 0648 London Euston-Plymouth rail tour. The GWR enthusiasts will say it is a 'Castle' pulling an A4, the LNER brigade will say it an 'A4' pushing a 'Castle.' A debate that will for ever rumble on. Such a combination would have been unknown in the steam era. *11 September 2010*

ABOVE: Moving slightly along to the north side of Embankment Road bridge, we have a peaceful and tranquil scene as an unidentified Class 47 diesel makes its way along the loop-line towards Tavistock Junction. In the foreground a lovely view of Blagdon's Boatyard with Laira Wharf on the left. Notice especially the little crane, and the boatyard which seems to be at capacity. The River Plym and Saltram Park make a lovely backdrop. This is indeed an image sure to conjure up many memories. *12 October 1970*

ABOVE: A summer's evening at Laira at high tide as 'Warship' Class diesel D855 'Triumph' heads light engine along the main line for Plymouth Station. The signal to the far left which D855 has just gone past is interesting with both arms in the 'off' position. The top one is the 'Down Home' signal for Laira Junction with the lower one the former Lipson Junction distant, taken over by the Plymouth Power Box, whose first colour light would be passed at Lipson Junction. The boatyard does not look as busy on this occasion, perhaps the sailors were taking advantage of the weather for a trip out. The vessel nearest the camera was a familiar sight here many years, and was, as far as I know, a former Naval Pinnace. *June 1967*

LAIRA BLAGDON'S BOAT YARD

BELOW: Now and then the railway photographer has a bit of luck and gets that perfect pass. This was unplanned and is a case of being in the right place at the right time. I had gone out for 'Western' Class D1048 'Western Lady' working 6V33 0427 Stoke-On-Trent-St Blazey seen here approaching Laira Junction on its way via Friary Yard. With perfect timing, D1010 'Western Campaigner came the other way with 4A13 1522 Penzance-Paddington vans - the leading vehicle being an empty sleeping car being worked back to London. What made this piece of luck even more remarkable was the 'Westerns' were reducing in number by the week. A transformed scene from where, not so long ago, there existed here the little Laira tidal inlet and Blagdon's Boatyard. *6 September 1976*

BELOW: The updated view of the present-day is dominated by the growth of vegetation, which does nothing to enhance the scene. Did Laira and its boatyard ever really exist? 'Voyager' 221 128 passes by with 1S55 1425 Plymouth - Edinburgh. *3 August 2013*

LAIRA WHARF

BELOW: We finish our somewhat in-depth study of Laira and the inlet and the boatyard by swinging the camera around to the left a little to show Laira Wharf, not to be confused with its larger neighbour by the Laira Bridge. This is where, at first the Plymouth & Dartmoor Railway (later taken over by the Lee Moor Tramway) ran, and, many years ago, china clay was transhipped from horse-worked wagons to sea-going craft. The latter doubtless somewhat restricted after 1848 when the main line was built creating the Causeway. Plenty of boats on show in Blagdon's Boatyard and I think I am correct in saying the black corrugated buildings were the workshops and offices. Parked on the former Tramway is a Mk 2 Ford Cortina registered in 1965. Perhaps this is best described as a tranquil scene by the River Plym. *12 October 1970*

BELOW: It is very difficult trying to work out what was exactly where these days, but pacing out from the main railway line north a few yards, going by a certain amount of memory and placing the back ground hills in the same place to the right of the bus stop, this is pretty close. I suspect many who travel along this road have no idea of what was sacrificed to build it. I suspect in years to come someone will say that they remember buses like that. Remember that today's photograph is tomorrow's history. *3 August 2013*

CRABTREE

BELOW: When the signals are cleared for the passage of the train, the railway term for this is 'boards off,' so we have one board off, and in the opposite direction comes a bus. The signal in this case is the 'Up' Advance Starter for Laira Junction signal box with the lower arm for Tavistock Junction Signal Box still at caution. The bus is Plymouth Corporation MCO 258H Fleet number 258, one of the Leyland Atlanteans built with the additional centre door for driver-only operation, a feature being introduced at around this time by many bus operators. The main road at this point is yet to be made into the wide expanse of carriageways we know so well today. The two-year-old twin viaducts of the Plympton Bypass show up well in the background - they had by now become an established local landmark. *10 November 1973*

BELOW: A fortunate gap between lamp posts coinciding with a clear patch in the growth provides a very similar vantage point today. I was hoping a bus would come along at the same time as the train! The main changes between the two images are really the background and the Plympton Bypass being obscured by the growth of trees. 153 325, one of the two green-liveried Class 153 single-car Sprinters (a welcome change from the corporate 'First' blue livery), hurries past with 2E46 1745 Plymouth-Exeter St Davids local service. *4 September 2013*

ABOVE: Plenty of interest and much to point out in this marvellous image of Class '03' diesel shunter D2140 heading away from Tavistock Junction Yard to Friary with a solitary brake van in tow. The view is from the main road with the former Bass Charrington Depot and Drake Carriers to the left. This site has now been taken over by the Sainsbury's Supermarket. In the former Crabtree rail sidings, installed as late as April 1964 as a single line with the ones either side being added in 1967, an ex-LMS passenger coach is stabled. I only wish that it could have stayed there until the Plym Valley Railway came on the scene. Look just beyond this and just visible in the gap between the trees is Lord Morley's Bridge, and, to the right, the open space whence the foot and bridle path lead to Saltram House. All of this now succeeded by the Plympton Bypass. The '03' is on the two way - i.e. can be used in either direction - loop between the Plym Viaduct and Laira Junction which is still in use today. All the signals were replaced by colour lights with the extension of the Plymouth Panel Box in November 1973. *August 1968*

LEFT: I wish I could present a similar updated view today as it would be very different. There is not a single place in amongst the growth and the trees to find anywhere to update the scene. Sainsbury's and the Plympton Bypass are behind the trees somewhere. *4 September 2013*

BRIDGES OVER AND BESIDE THE PLYM

RIGHT: Taken from a passing train with the front of it crossing the Plym Viaduct, a last look at Lord Morley's Bridge as this and the embankment to the right are under going demolition to make way for the construction of the Plympton Bypass. Note, to the extreme left, the double bracket signal, the right-hand board off for the main line, the left-hand one was for the 'Up' Loop, but prior to the 1965 extension of the latter, it was for the branch to Tavistock South and Launceston. *August 1968*

RIGHT: A view from the other side of the track and a bit closer in as 'Peak' D52 brings 1V76 0910 Liverpool-Plymouth under the then two-year-old Plympton Bypass where Lord Morley's Bridge once stood and over the River Plym. The signal has lost its left arm with disconnection of the former 'Up' Loop at this point. *30 October 1973*

RIGHT: The scene has changed again, rather dramatically, with another tier added to the A38 at this point, the Marsh Mills Flyover completed in 1992. The original twin viaducts of the Plympton Bypass then became slip roads, and they were replaced in 1995 after suffering concrete cancer. Other than the loss of the signal, it's a case of the railway still here with everything else around it having changed. 'Sprinter' 153 325 comes under the A38 and over the River Plym with 2P93 1605 Exeter St Davids-Plymouth local service. *4 September 2013*

PLYM VIADUCT – SOUTHERN SIDE

BELOW: A clear view looking down the Plym Estuary from the new bridge built for the footpath to Saltram, it gave a higher elevation than Lord Morley's Bridge. 'Western' class D1054 'Western Governor' passes by with 1A69 0835 Penzance-Paddington, the Alfred Bell depot is to the right, behind is the bracket signal with the arm cleared for a 'Down' train to take the each way loop. The new colour-light which would replace it within a fortnight is right opposite. Bass Charrington and the Crabtree Sidings are then visible, with the roadworks to widen the A374 in full swing. *30 October 1973*

BELOW: I just had to include this one to show the changes in the intermediate years as the engine hauling the 0730 Penzance - Glasgow/Aberdeen is 50 017 'Royal Oak', which is now preserved just around the corner from here on the Plym Valley Railway. I never thought, then, that this engine would have such a close association with the River Plym. The engine is carrying the later 'Network South East' livery, the sector created to over see the London and South East area. It was not uncommon to see this livery down here, and being used on Cross Country trains to Birmingham. Everything then was 'common user,' without all the fuss and ado about leasing, hiring and all the elements that make up today's accountant's railway - a legacy of political interference in the industry. Back to the picture, biggest change is the retaining wall in the background, built to protect the now-widened A379, and from here it does look quite a substantial structure. *31 January 1987*

PLYM VIADUCT - SOUTHERN SIDE

BELOW: A decade after the 'Royal Oak' picture, the scene on the right beside the railway line has changed very substantially. Gone are Alfred Bell's Depot, Bass Charrington, and the Crabtree Sidings and all else to make way for Sainsbury's and its car park. Look also how the vegetation has sprung up behind, with the retaining wall for the main road hardly visible. A real decade of change, yet the railway has altered little. On the rails, 'Class 60' 60 030 passes by with the 0940 Burngullow-Alexandra Dock Junction (Newport, South Wales). These engines were the last class to be built for the unified British Rail, and their heyday in the West Country was short. Privatisation has been unkind to the Class with some withdrawn and many stored out of use particularly at Toton. *19 August 1998*

BELOW: The scene as seen at present with the Plym Viaduct receiving some attention. The Sainsbury's sign is more visible, but due to the growth, little else can be seen of the surrounding area. The railway itself is still the same, a classic example of all around it being the subject of change. 43098 with 43124 on the rear power along with 1A85 1255 Plymouth-Paddington. *4 September 2013.*

PLYM VIADUCT – FROM THE NORTH

LEFT: In the pre-Plympton Bypass era, the view of the Plym Viaduct on the north side was a bit restricted. Taken from the footpath which led to Lord Morley's Bridge, Class '03' D2178 heads for Tavistock Junction with oil from the Cattewater Branch and general freight from Friary. *August 1968*

LEFT: One benefit which I am sure the road planners did not envisage was that the Plympton Bypass gave a higher elevation than Lord Morley's Bridge which it superseded, and a thus a much better angle for railway photography. Every cloud has a silver lining. The anglers who seem to be in a rather precarious position on the Viaduct – and an illegal one at that as this is trespass – are disturbed by the passing of 'Western' class D1013 'Western Ranger' with the 6M55 St. Blazey to Stoke-On-Trent with a neat line of clay hoods behind the engine. The notice on the right is to inform the passing public they are passing 'Alfred Bell Storage and Distribution' *13 July 1976*

LEFT: 'Alfred Bell' and the firms in this part of Crabtree are no more, Sainsbury's supermarket now occupying the site. There is little evidence now from this angle of the present-day use of this land as, like the rest of the view, the scene is spoilt by the ever-increasing spread of vegetation. The view behind the train where, with D1013, we see the River Plym and Saltram has been completely obliterated. An unidentified First Great Western HST heads away towards London. This view is totally impossible now. *July 2008*

TAVISTOCK JUNCTION

BELOW: The view from Lord Morley's Bridge looking east as 'Western' Class D1030 'Western Musketeer' heads around the curve from the Marshalling Yard with 1C55 1230 Paddington-Penzance. To the extreme left, the little stone building was the original signal box of, I believe, mid-1870s construction. This was just knocked down one day, not long after this photograph was taken. The formation of the double track which took the Tavistock and Launceston Branch around to Marsh Mills Station is clearly visible: beyond that is a well-stocked freight yard with the houses of Woodford behind. *August 1968.*

BELOW: Only three years later and still very much in the 'Western' era, a new vantage point has emerged in the shape of the Plympton Bypass which superseded Lord Morley's Bridge, and gave a higher and wider vantage point. This was, for me, when the London trains were at their zenith. A very smart D1049 'Western Monarch' only five days out of Swindon Works rounds the curve past Tavistock Junction Signal Box with a very smart rake of mostly Mark II coaches forming 1B25 0830 Paddington-Penzance. Tavistock Junction Marshalling Yard was still busy place back then with plenty of traffic, the sidings in the 'Up' yard are well-stocked with wagons. *2 November 1971*

LEFT: The years had not dealt kindly with the railway scene here. The signal box was closed on 10 November 1973 when the area was placed under the control of Plymouth Panel Signal Box. With a combination of the freight traffic draining away, and the introduction of more modern and larger, higher-capacity wagons, the freight train of short open and covered wagons with a brake van belongs to another age. Hence the reduction of traffic using the Marshalling Yard, which has shrunk a little with the expansion of the pallet yard on the left, and in the background the construction of an industrial unit. On the right, the track work from the 'Down' yard has either been lifted or left to rot in the weeds. There is also the usual expansion in the general growth of trees and vegetation. A throw back to the past as preserved 'King' 6024 King Edward I passes with 1Z24 0530 Paddington-Penance rail tour. *19 September 1998*

LEFT: I was pleasantly surprised to walk up to here for an updated shot expecting the view to be blocked even more by further growth, only to find the view off the Plympton Bypass is, by today's standards, quite open. There has been further growth, and it's doubtful that any trains will ever again use the former 'down' lines on the right. 'Topps Tiles' occupy the industrial building behind the Marshalling Yard which now sees very limited use and is devoid of wagons. Sadly, no freight whatsoever comes to Plymouth by rail these days. How green is that? One for the environmental brigade to get their heads around. 43185 front and 43010 rear are seen with 1C79 1106 Paddington-Plymouth. *6 August 2013*

ST BONIFACE ARENA

ABOVE: Not the normal angle off the Plympton Bypass, one taken at the time to show the formation of the curve of the former GWR Tavistock and Launceston Branch from the main line before it passed under the former A38 and into Marsh Mills Station. This stands out well behind 'Peak' D26 with 1E54 1512 Plymouth-Leeds, note the buffet vehicle is right behind the engine, I think this came off at Sheffield. Behind the latter we see a real slice of life with a school rugby match in progress, the little grandstand has few spectators. Behind the playing field a clear view of the houses in Plymouth Road before the era of McDonalds, Comet and Curry's. The Clay Works can be seen in the distance on the hill. In the foreground note the new road as part of the construction of the sewerage farm, something most residents of the area wish had never happened. *30 October 1973*

BELOW: This is the corresponding view today: there is little other than the background hills to link the two images. Regrettably there is no smoke any more coming from the now-closed clay works. The former A38 road-bridge (since extended) that the GWR Tavistock Branch passed beneath, can just be spotted on the far right, the original now blocked by its concrete neighbour. Where the rugby was being played is now the St Boniface Arena, home of the Plymouth Devils Speedway but one would never know it from this angle. It is hard even to pick out the main line as Class 150 'Sprinter' 150 126 attached to 153 361 heads along with 2A63 1141 Penzance-Newton Abbot. *6 August 2013*

LONGBRIDGE

ABOVE: What must be the oldest surviving railway structures after Leigham Tunnel (1823) in the city, and, more than likely, anywhere else in the West Country, is the little iron bridge constructed in 1829 to take the Cann Quarry Branch of the horse-drawn Plymouth & Dartmoor Railway over the River Plym. From 1854 this was also used by the Lee Moor Tramway which joined the Cann Quarry Line near Plym Bridge, and was incorporated into the latter when the P&D ceased operations in 1900. A delightful view from what was then the A38 road bridge in Plymouth Road, on the left notice the old-style 30 mph restriction sign which I think makes the picture. Weighbridge Cottage is to the right. It is indeed quite a rural scene, but it's odd to see cars parked up on the waste ground that is now the Coypool Park and Ride site. *August 1968*

ABOVE: The former A38 here became the B3416 when the Plympton Bypass opened in 1970, and that is not the only change here as the view has largely been surrendered to the growth of the trees that now crowd the foreground. The little bridge is hardly visible and we can see nothing of Coypool behind. The 30 mph sign has been replaced by a 7.5 ton weight restriction board which also carries the one-way sign and the cycle-path indicator. I suspect that of those who cross the Plym here in their cars, few probably realise what history is beside them. *6 August 2013*

LONGBRIDGE

RIGHT: The Lee Moor Tramway on its route out from Plymouth made a very acute right-hand turn to cross Longbridge Road, before reaching the little iron bridge which took it across the River Plym. Note the 'check' rail installed to prevent derailments. This is one of the sharpest bends I have seen on a railway and/or mineral line. *August 1968*

RICHT: There is no evidence here at all that the Tramway once crossed the road here. The scene is cluttered with temporary buildings erected for use by workers in connection with restoration of the bridge, so this scene is liable to change but is will still leave no evidence of the railway here. Look just behind the traffic bollard and the little wall on the end of the iron bridge, and that provides a common link between the images. *6 August 2013*

ABOVE: The view from the Longbridge Road looking east over the iron bridge with the rails in place, a scene which had probably changed little over the years. Weighbridge Cottage is to the left. On the opposite side of the river, the Cann Quarry Branch/Lee Moor Tramway can be seen taking a left turn for the curve around to Coypool. This was the junction for the Plymouth & Dartmoor Plympton Branch opened in 1834, which went straight on, its course eradicated by the field and buildings beyond. The Longridge does not look in the best condition, the railings best described as looking quite rickety. *August 1968*

ABOVE: The Longbridge has now passed into the care of the National Trust and is listed as a scheduled ancient monument, so its future is assured. The track has long since gone, but the general view is almost the same. Weighbridge Cottage on the left has lost a chimney and changed colour with some further external alterations, but is still has that old-world charm about it. The Longbridge is currently being restored with support from the cycle and footpaths charity, Sustrans. Over recent years, with storms and floods, many of the stones in the bridge's abutments have gone missing or been badly damaged. Some have been salvaged from the River Plym, others replaced with material sourced locally. Stonemason, Mark Robinson and his team are doing an excellent job which, when complete, will keep this iconic structure in good repair, hopefully for many years to come. *6 August 2013*

PLYMOUTH & DARTMOOR RAILWAY – PLYMPTON BRANCH

The Plympton Branch of the Plymouth & Dartmoor Railway opened in 1834, was bought by the South Devon Railway in 1947 and closed to avoid competition when their own line in to Plymouth was opened in 1848. The Plympton Branch of the P&D after Marsh Mills Works was built on an embankment alongside the Plymouth Eastern Turnpike road. This later became the A38 until the opening of the Plympton Bypass in 1970 when it became demoted to the B3416. The traffic it carries today as a 'B' road is far heavier than that it carried as an 'A' road. I wonder how many people travelling along the road to Plympton realise that the elevated footpath is a relic of a horse-drawn tramway, one of the earliest line closures in the country.

RIGHT TOP: Plymouth Road looking east towards Plympton when it was the A38 with typical 1960s volume of traffic. St Mary's Bridge is in the far background. *August 1968*

RIGHT: Forty-five years later the road has seen a few changes, so has the level of traffic. More traffic signs have appeared, there is more white paint around and the trees have grown, but there is still much to link the two images. *6 August 2013*

ABOVE: A further view from the south side of the road; it was much easier to cross then. The elevation of the pavement is quite marked here. A quiet 'A' road featuring one of many red Millbay Laundry vans that were once such a common sight in the city. *August 1968*

ABOVE: I cannot come up with a Millbay Laundry van these days, a blue van and a traffic island will have to do. A convenient break in the traffic shows how the road has changed and how much more busy it is. There is no obvious railway connection in any of the pictures, but that raised embankment which carries the footpath is a real railway relic and one of the oldest at that. Take time to study it next time you go past. *6 August 2013*

COT HILL LOOKING WEST

ABOVE: The Cot Hill over-bridge was, in its time, a good location for railway photography, the only snag on the west side being the narrow pavement, which can make life difficult with present-day traffic levels. No such problems back in 1970 with 'Western' Class diesel D1011 'Western Thunderer' running light engine towards Plymouth. This is, of course, also the view of the eastern end of Tavistock Junction Yard and back at this time, both the 'Up' to the right and 'Down' to the left yards were in operation. Just look at the size of it and the amount of rolling stock on view, especially the 'Down' Yard with, I think, 14 parallel sidings running the whole length of the place. In the far distance, beyond the signal box and the signals, the eagle-eyed can pick out the brand new Plympton Bypass. *9 December 1970*

ABOVE: It does not take very long in some cases for change to become apparent. Four and a quarter years on from 1011 passing by, we see another rare and historic visitor to the city in the shape of the prototype High Speed Train, the only Class 252 set to have been built, passing Tavistock Junction Yard. Look to the left and those once packed sidings are now empty and rusting away for much of the 'Down' Yard had closed not that long before. One certainly gets an impression of just how vast the 'Down 'Yard really was. *March 1975*

COT HILL LOOKING WEST

BELOW: Wind on not far short of a quarter of a century and the scene has seen a great deal of change. The former 'Down' Yard is no more, passing into non-railway use. There had been further life for one of the sidings on the 'Down' side when in the 1980s it gained a purpose built rail-served depot for Ushers (of Trowbridge) Brewery, but, as can be seen, this had become disused by this time, as yet more freight traffic had moved away from rail. In the 'Up' Yard a new wagon repair shed has appeared, and some of the land to the right has been sold of for industrial use. Heading east is another now gone, long-standing train, 66 052 has charge of 6S55 0940 Burngullow-Irvine clay slurry. This train used to run twice a week. The clay slurry still goes to Irvine by rail, but comes across the ocean on a boat from Brazil to Antwerp in Belgium. Then it is loaded into the familiar tanks, the train is worked through the Channel Tunnel to form 6S94 Dollands Moor-Irvine via the West Coast Main Line. This apparently is cheaper then getting the clay slurry from Cornwall. I remain unconvinced. *27 March 2002*

BELOW: The almost depressing scene today of a once busy installation now totally rundown and showing signs of neglect. The only traffic in the yard amongst the weeds is one empty fuel tank and five China clay wagons in transit from Cornwall to the Potteries. 'Voyager' 221 129 hurries past with 1S55 1325 Plymouth-Edinburgh. *30 November 2011*

COT HILL LOOKING EAST

ABOVE: Time was when the area around Cot Hill looked quite rural, although the activity in the background would suggest development of the field to the left of the railway has only recently commenced. Just after passing the fine three-arm bracket signal, the Tavistock Junction 'Down' Home with the route set for the main line, 'Hymek' D 7049 passes with 1Z01 Inspection special. Of the Hydraulic Classes, the Hymeks although not rare visitors, were certainly not, by this time, a daily sight. *17 July 1969*

BELOW: There is much similarity between the two images with a clear view up the line towards Plympton. On the right, the 'Down' loop from St Mary's Bridge is still there but is now a long siding from Tavistock Junction. On the left the former 'Up' Loop and 'Departure' lines have been slewed to form a dead end siding. The wide open field on the left has indeed been developed and is now the Queensway Store. A rare visitor to Plymouth in the form of 'Class 56' 56 043 pilots 'Class 47' 560 on their way, I think, to a Laira Open Day. *May 1982*

COT HILL LOOKING EAST

ABOVE: The former 'Down' loop and the remains of the 'Up' loop and Departure road are still there, but the foliage has grown making the scene rather untidy. The Queensway building has turned blue and there is further development beyond this. This was still the era when there were still some locomotive-hauled trains on the London route, they would last for another couple of years. First Great Western liveried 47 813 has charge of the 1233 Paddington-Penzance. Of particular interest are the two motorail vans on the front, a short-lived attempt to revive the service insisted upon by politicians as part of the franchise agreement. This was a short-lived feature. *16 June 2000*

BELOW: Like so many other scenes we have witnessed through out this book, this yet another one where the railway track remains and looks familiar but the overall view has been compromised by the runaway growth of vegetation, almost completely hiding the former Queensway building. One can still pick out a part of Plympton in the background, but this is far from the original clear scene of 1970. A rear view of 'Voyager' 221 134 heading away from the city with 1S53 1324 Plymouth-Edinburgh. Our next port of call St Mary's Bridge is just around the corner. *6 August 2013*

PLYMPTON ST MARY'S BRIDGE LOOKING WEST.

LEFT: This is probably one of the rarest shots one will ever see of a 'Western' Class Diesel. The Blue Pullman Diesel Sets, often regarded as the forerunners of the High Speed Train, were not seen west of Bristol, except on a couple of occasions when one was chartered for a 'Holiday Inn' Christmas Special from, and back to, London for at least two years running. They were under-powered for the South Devon banks and, as an act of insurance, D1032 'Western Marksman' has been attached to pilot the Pullman set as far as Newton Abbot. This is a very unusual combination. It is not often one sees Plympton looking more like an Arctic wasteland, but looking west from St Mary's Bridge one can still take in the view looking back towards Cot Hill. 1Z03 Plymouth -Paddington *28 December 1970.*

LEFT: The original view point is not now possible due to growth, lack of a footway – standing on St Mary's Bridge this side nowadays is a bit hazardous, and the 1980s provision of a footbridge which blocks the view anyway. So it is to this footbridge we adjourn in much warmer conditions to see the train still crossing the Tory Brook at this point, the concrete bridge was installed after the 1960 flooding and has kept the railway dry here ever since. 47 736 front and 47 774 rear pass with 1Z14 1124 Plymouth-Exeter Riverside 'Serco' departmental special *24 May 2001.*

LEFT: It is still possible, just, to get the shot here but like so many others, it is the rampant growth which has over taken the scene, thus blocking most of the view. 43169 front with 43133 on the rear speed their way through Plympton with 1A85 1047 Penzance-Paddington *6 August 2013*

PLYMPTON ST MARY'S BRIDGE LOOKING EAST – PLYMPTON GOODS YARD.

ABOVE: Looking east from St Mary's Bridge and we have 'Western' Class D1005 'Western Venturer' nearing the end of its journey with 1B39 1040 Paddington-Plymouth. With only three months and a few days to go before the last of the Class were withdrawn, 'Westerns' were in short supply by now, but this train was one of the few one could rely on to produce 'a 1000' as they were also known, hence my many pilgrimages out to see this train at this period. It was to the west side of the Plym Bridge Road over-bridge that the goods yard for the former Plympton station was situated, and the site of the latter, closed on 1 June 1964, is to the right of the train. This, however, was not the first use of this site for goods traffic. Of historic interest is the old building to the far right that once formed part of the terminus of the Plymouth & Dartmoor Railway Plympton Branch, which was bought and closed by the South Devon Railway to avoid competition. In the days of the horse and cart, with roads nothing like those we know today, it was a tortuous journey for the clay and other produce coming down from Lee Moor and surrounding area to the wharfs in Plymouth, so the 1834 provision of a tramway here had an immediate effect, transhipment onto the primitive horse-worked line greatly speeding up the process. This is why the South Devon Railway wanted the traffic on their line. *21 October 1976*

ABOVE: All trace of the Plympton Goods Yard with its former role as the terminus of the P&D Plympton Branch has been swept away by housing development on the site. Excessive growth does not help so I had to alter the position from the original slightly so as not to just provide a view of trees. A rear end view of 'Sprinter' 150 263 working 2A99 1532 Plymouth-Newton Abbot. *3 August 2013*

PLYMPTON STATION

ABOVE: The view looking east from the Plym Bridge Road over-bridge shows the site of Plympton Station which closed to passengers 3 March 1959. The main line curves away to the ascent of Hemerdon Bank to leave the city. One can only ponder how useful an eight minute train journey from here in to Plymouth would be these days, avoiding the motorist's nightmare that is Marsh Mills Roundabout and the three that would apply also to traffic from Plymstock: Gdynia Way, Cattedown Roundabout and Exeter Street. Who knows how long it will be before someone in authority recognises the benefits of providing facilities for passengers to board some of the trains which come hurtling through here. The station was demolished not that long after closure but the formation of the platforms is clearly visible. To the left, by Boringdon Road, the gap between hedge and fence marks the entrance to the former station. On the right on the former 'down' platform the signal box remained in use until taken over by the Plymouth Panel late in 1973. To the far right we see a brand new Glen Road with the development of the adjacent area yet to happen. I remember Dr Tom Forest, one of the original members of the Plymouth Railway Circle, asking at a meeting if we noted the new photographic opportunities created by the new road and clear view by Plympton station? *Late 1960s*

ABOVE: I wonder what Dr Forest would make of the tree-laden view today. 43021 front and 43092 rear hurry past with no evidence of the station remaining with 1C84 1306 Paddington-Penzance *3 August 2013*

THE NEW MARSH MILLS

The Great Western Tavistock and Launceston Branch is a separate story, and will be the subject of a further volume, but one small part of this former line within the city boundary has been restored from nothing by the Plym Valley Railway, becoming the jewel in the crown of the story of Plymouth and its railways. We pay a brief visit to examine this remarkable transformation.

RIGHT: The way things were. Looking north from Marsh Mills towards Tavistock, at the junction with the 1940-built short branch to the MOD Depot at Coypool. The rusting and little-used Bickleigh Siding was a retained short stretch of the Branch closed at the end of 1962. *October 1972*

LEFT: The Plym Valley Railway Association was formed in 1980 with the aim of restoring the section of line from Marsh Mills to Plym Bridge. Access to the then scrub woodland site adjacent to Coypool was gained early in 1982. After a period of negotiation, the PVR purchased the Bickleigh Siding in 1988 and this became the site for the new station. A much-changed scene from the above (the background trees link the two images) as work is under way to level the elevation of the railway prior to the construction of the new Marsh Mills Station. Under restoration, the then PVR Association-owned former BR Standard 4 75079, the last of its class numerically, is reflected in a puddle. *15 November 1992*

LEFT: The brand-new finished product, and yes it does look very smart, a tribute to John Netherton and Bill Ross who led the construction team. All the mud is gone, a new station, a new line with superbly laid track, and we can still link the three pictures by the background trees. As I write these words, work is now underway to extend the Platform further south and this will then accommodate the former Billacombe station building. Welcome to the Plym Valley Railway. *4 March 2001*

MARSH MILLS NORTH JUNCTION LOOKING SOUTH

LEFT: The formation of the Tavistock Branch is on the extreme left and parked on a very short length of rail is 75079 then not long out of Barry scrap-yard, in front of which is the buffer-stop denoting the northern limit of the Bickleigh Siding. The latter was still owned by British Rail, who at the time were reluctant to sell it, even though they had no practical use for it. Purchase of this was completed in 1988. To the right is the cutting made by the PVR to link the newly established base at Marsh Mills to the former branch. 75079 was subsequently sold to the Mid-Hants Railway where restoration work continues. Another of the engines bought from Barry is Bulleid Pacific 34007 'Wadebridge' seen on the right. This engine subsequently moved away to Bodmin for completion of restoration and is now based on the Mid-Hants although it has graced some of the other major preserved lines around the country with a visit. More high-quality Plym Valley mud is on offer. *29 April 1983*

BELOW: The much-improved and mud-free view today, a credit to the fine work of the volunteers who built the PVR. 'Albert' is scattering the autumn leaves as this fine little engine pounds up the bank out of Marsh Mills Station pulling the two-coach DMU in use as coaching stock, and for comparison purposes both 'Albert' and 75079 in the picture above are in the same position. The line to the right serves as access to the carriage and storage sidings, workshop and locomotive shed. The next page features the view from the top of the bank between the two engines looking north towards the photographer. *1 November 2009*

MARSH MILLS NORTH JUNCTION LOOKING NORTH

BELOW: All we had when came on site at Marsh Mills to start the long task of building a base and restoring the line to Plym Bridge was the remaining stretch of the Bickleigh Siding. This is to the right being the formation of the Branch to Tavistock and Launceston. Everything else had to be built ourselves from nothing, the task was long and hard, the labourers were few, but what a fine bunch they have been over the years ... and the finances were tight. Marsh Mills North Junction is a pure Plym Valley Railway creation. This view is looking North, I am stood on the bank that was reduced in height. The land to the left was cleared from waste scrub and on the left edge, levels raised considerably to attain enough room for the line in to our base and the required head shunt. And then people ask why the project took so long. Plenty of work still to be done here. The gloomy Friday before the gloomy August Bank Holiday weekend of 1988!

BELOW: North Junction looks as if has it has always been there, but in the days when this was the Tavistock and Launceston Branch, the only line that existed here was the one to the right. Every thing else is the work of the PVR. By far the largest and certainly the most powerful engine ever to work on the Tavistock Branch, the magnificently restored 50 017 'Royal Oak' in its original Network South East livery (compare with the shot if 50 017 crossing the Plym Viaduct) trundles through, with the oldest working Class 08 Diesel Shunter in the Country 13002 is just visible to the left. *9 June 2012*

WORLD'S END

No, I have not got these in the wrong order. The 'Then' image is the one of an abandoned former railway with a crumbling little over-bridge, and the 'Now' image is the one of the well-kept railway running up through the valley.

LEFT: One of the obstacles to restoration of the line was the condition of three over-bridges: to cut a long story short the Buildings & Works team had to spend a great deal of time in their restoration. For many years, it seemed like restoration would never get past the first bridge for this was a challenge on a different scale. Then there were things like fencing, by law every railway has to be, where practicable, fenced for safety reasons, and a glance to the bottom right shows the new fence is already there, but this again had been months and months of painstaking work. Track creeping up the valley can be seen in the back ground, but for a long time this would be the limit of our railway, the end of our little world, hence at first the nick name 'World's End' which became a symbol of the challenge to finish the job. The name has now become official – and permanent. *18 March 1998.*

ABOVE: After about three years of work on bridge the rebuilding and re-pointing was finished, together with the laying of track and more fencing. This allowed the Plym Valley to reach another milestone. The Railway officially re-opened for passenger traffic from the new Marsh Mills Station to World's End in October 2001, and in May 2008 at long last went beyond World's End when the line was extended to Lee Moor Crossing. 'Albert' and the three superbly restored BR Mark 2 coaches give us this wonderful portrait of 'The Woodland Line' at World's End Bridge. *25 September 2011*

LEE MOOR CROSSING

RIGHT: The Saturdays-only 1240 Launceston-Plymouth, known as 'The Argyle Train' passing the site of Lee Moor Crossing with an unidentified 4575 Class Prairie tank in charge. The view is from the Lee Moor Tramway (originally at this point the Cann Quarry Tramway - until closure of the latter in 1900) which diagonally crossed the Tavistock and Launceston Branch on the level at this point. On the left, behind the derelict, permanent, way-hut, are the remains of the former 'Lee Moor Crossing Signal Box' which was closed in January 1955: however as far as I know no traffic had passed over the Tramway at this point since 1947. *March 1962*

RIGHT: The same view some 20 years later. The course of the former branch to Tavistock and Launceston (closed at the end of 1962 and demolished here in mid-1964) is clearly defined, and the diagonal path of the former Tramway can be discerned. Here we see yet another abandoned railway. *10 June 1983*

RIGHT: The Lee Moor Tramway had been by now converted in to a cycle path, so it would be necessary to cross this at the same point for the Plym Valley to finish its extension to Plym Bridge. Work has just got under way on the new facility where the cycle path was amended slightly to cross the railway line on a straight alignment with traditional wooden crossing gates crafted by John Netherton and his team. There is work afoot on the once abandoned railway in the woods. *26 April 2009*

RIGHT: The railway is restored with the view from the new Lee Moor Crossing of 13002 on the front and 'Albert' on the rear as the second train from the newly opened Plym Bridge Platform makes its way back to Marsh Mills. 51 years of photography in the same spot - remarkable. *30 December 2012*

PLYM BRIDGE PLATFORM

ABOVE: Just prior to the lifting of the track, the disused Plym Bridge Platform looking towards Marsh Mills. The line from Tavistock Junction through here to Tavistock was opened 22 June 1859 (the extension to Launceston on 1 July 1865). It was not until 1 May 1906 a station was provided here to serve the local beauty spot, the name taken from the nearby road bridge over the river, and was originally of wooden construction. In October 1949 the station was shortened by about 100 feet and replaced by a new structure of built of concrete which served until closure (31 December 1962). The structure was removed from here (by road) to form part of the new St Ives Station in Cornwall opened 23 May 1971, built on the end of Porthminster Viaduct to allow the original station site to become a lucrative car park, so when one alights at St Ives, one could say one is alighting at Plym Bridge Platform! I apologise for this picture not being quite the quality one would expect, I could only afford a roll of black and white film in the family Box Brownie camera at the time. *May 1964*

ABOVE: After removal of the little station in 1970, this is how it then looked for many years with the end rails rusting away by the one small piece of it that remained, and the foundations clearly visible beside the empty track bed. In many cases of a closed and long demolished railway and station, this was the end of the story. This tale has a happy ending. *22 February 2009*

PLYM BRIDGE PLATFORM

BELOW: 'Resurgam' – I will rise again – to take a quote from St Andrew's, the Mother Church of Plymouth so badly damaged by enemy action in the bombing of Plymouth in the Second World War. The site has been cleared, work is under way on the track bed with new sleepers in position to herald the return of the rails, and the new Plym Bridge Platform built in concrete and with a length more similar to the first station here, rises from above the foundations its predecessor, another masterpiece and much hard work by the Buildings & Works team. Not only did they have to build the station, ground had to be levelled, the footpath to it realigned and rebuilt and then there was all the work on the fence opposite at the bottom of the bank by the meadow. I cannot overstate the hard work by the track gang in relaying the line, this shot illustrates just how pain staking it is to rebuild a railway line. So much has been done by so few to bring back this once abandoned stretch of 'The Branch'. *20 February 2011*

BELOW: The inaugural train at Plym Bridge Platform reopened 50 years to the day it closed. What an achievement to conclude this book with a story of dereliction and removal, and then replacement and rebirth. As the Founder Member of the Plym Valley Railway, I was given the honour of reopening the new Plym Bridge Platform. There are no words or superlatives that can fully explain my sheer joy and delight in representing the volunteers at such a culmination of their dedicated work over so many years. Plymouth take note – here is something special for the City to enjoy. *30 December 2012*